EKSTASIS

"BE·MUCH OCCUPIED
WITH
JESUS"

SEA HARP PRESS

Bordering Kingdoms

Bordering Kingdoms

Toward a New Aesthetic of Christian Art and Living

EKSTASIS authors with foreword by Conor Sweetman

If I imagined two kingdoms bordering each other, one of which I knew rather well and the other not at all, and if however much I desired it I was not allowed to enter the unknown kingdom, I would still be able to form some idea of it. I would go to the border of the kingdom known to me and follow it all the way, and in doing so I would by my movements describe the outline of that unknown land and thus have a general idea of it, although I had never set foot in it. And if this was a labor that occupied me very much, if I was unflaggingly scrupulous, it presumably would sometimes happen that as I stood with sadness at the border of my kingdom and gazed longingly into that unknown country that was so near and yet so far, I would be granted an occasional little disclosure.

Søren Kierkegaard

Either/Or

CONTENTS

FOREWORD

THERE IS A TONE THAT'S CHANGING in the ways we communicate, as it always does. Generations grow up, new vocabularies come into use, and cultures evolve in their aesthetic and emotional atmosphere. The sands of time shift beneath our feet and bring new diamonds and grit to the shore with every decade that passes. For all the confusion of our current day, all the lament of how politics and technology is changing our expectations of our souls and each other, I believe that there is a poetic impulse that lies just beneath the surface of human history—the eternal draw toward the "true myth"—that is swelling and longing to break upon the shores of our stultified attentions.

Recognizing the intricate interplay between mediums and messages, we acknowledge that our bodies and minds are primed for a profound and transformative exchange, even in weak-willed times. Whether it was Gutenberg's printing press or Jack Dorsey's Twitter, the tone of communication may change, but the essence of the human soul remains remarkably consistent throughout the ages.

The breaking waves and swelling depths reach us as we come to a clearer, more visceral understanding of the spiritual dryness and diseases that have been creeping up for a long while. As we confront the wounds and wickedness of our world, we stand on the precipice of a great healing.

In the midst of a changing landscape, we yearn for a language that speaks to our souls in a diffuse and dispersed manner, acknowledging and embracing our intricacies without reducing them to commodities. The core of our *Imago Dei*-shaped reality gives us hints and ideas of this new language, and I believe a poetic lens of life begins to illuminate the shapes in the distance of that other kingdom.

Bordering Kingdoms: Toward a New Aesthetic of Christian Art and Living is structured as a transformative journey into the heart of faithful, creative experience. Divided into four distinct parts—Revelation, Creation, Craft, and Criticism—we navigate the intricate web that connects these disciplines, understanding their vital importance within a thriving artistic ecosystem. Each discipline, in its unique way, allows us to enter and grow in the life of the artist, writer, and creator.

At the heart of Ekstasis lies the pursuit of a cutting-edge creativity: the timeless beauty of orthodoxy through a poetic lens of faith, skillful storytelling, and visual levity. As you enjoy this collection of works published over the past three years in *Ekstasis*, I hope *Bordering Kingdoms* invites you to transcend old frameworks, cultivate a deeper understanding of faithful aesthetics, and awaken your soul to the holy mundane. Let's journey together into the borderlands, where the earthly and the divine intermingle, and discover a new aesthetic frame that illuminates the path to a more vibrant and meaningful existence.

Conor Sweetman
Editor, *Ekstasis*

REVELATION

ETERNITY IN OUR HEART

Kelly Kruse

AS A CHILD AND YOUNG ADULT, I thought that I was home-sick for beauty itself. Like many artists, I was aware of a sort of insatiable hunger in me for the beautiful at an early age. I grew up in northwest Iowa, near a place called the Loess Hills, named for its glacially deposited bluffs of humus-rich yellow soil. The sunsets in those bluffs brought about some of my first experiences of transient beauty, too rich to savor all at once, a feast that disappears before it can be finished.

The view of the stars from the farm of my childhood tore a cavernous maw of longing in my heart. It is a gift I am still learning to receive. On a clear night in winter on the farm, where there is little light pollution, the cosmic dust of the milky way is visible in a sweeping band of hazy half-light across the black bowl of the heavens, inlaid with its innumerable stars. I've traveled to China and across Europe and seen many beautiful places, but there has been no place quite like that rural Iowa sky on a winter night to break down the door of my heart and let the longing pour out like a raging sea. I was being called home by the beauty of nature long before I set out into the world, but I know now that home in its deepest sense was never truly found in Northwest Iowa.

•••

Sehnsucht is a German word for a particular kind of longing that I have heard described as a homesickness for a place you've never been. You may ask, but how could we be homesick if we haven't been there? This is a good question, and it's also part of the secret. We have been there, in some sort of shared collective memory passed through genealogy, wisdom, and creativity. We all know that things are not as they should be, and one of the greatest thrusts behind human progress comes from a desire to fix these things and reach a sort of perfect world. For all of human history we've struggled to agree on how to get there, though all of us partake, at least at some point, in the illusion that we can fix it on our own terms.

When we experience Sehnsucht, we get some sort of a glimpse behind the doorway to that secret home and how it will feel to get there—to the place of perfection and beauty. This glimpse is pleasurable, but the sensation is bittersweet. It doesn't last, and the emptiness on the other end of the feeling can be profound. We are prone to think the memory or discovery of our truest self can be unburied somewhere from a childhood memory or in an experience of beauty, but those things are just vehicles for the longing, as C.S. Lewis so beautifully expressed in *The Weight of Glory*.

•••

The doors of the deep places in me were opened by art at a young age too. I cultivated a love for classical music as a middle schooler at a time when I was first vulnerable to the acute sensation of depression. When in the dark of my room, unsure of how to cope with the unbearable weight of existence, I slipped my headphones over my ears to let Tchaikovsky and Beethoven do their work on my soul. Deprived of visual stimuli, I would lay there in the dark, neurons firing and alive with harmony. The images would come to me unbidden then, and I began to paint to explore them around the same time. The invisible beauty and plumbless depths of classical music became a fixture in my life, giving me purpose, stimulation, and escape. The life-altering discoveries of particular works of music came to me regularly and come to me still, over twenty years later. Many of my most intense spiritual experiences have come through the unseen power of music.

One of my favorite composers is the German Romantic composer Johannes Brahms. The first time I sang the Brahms setting of Friedrich Schiller's poem "Nänie," I was fourteen. In sotto voce, I sang the words, "Even beauty must perish, and all the perfect must die," and Brahms's harmonic language made the hairs on the back of my neck stand up during every rehearsal. I lacked the experience to comprehend Schiller's poetry then, but the music conveyed its truth to me on a neurological level. I spent five hours or more a week singing in choir from the time I was twelve until I turned twenty-five. I've felt Sehnsucht in that space a remarkable amount of times, in the work of composers from every musical era. Making music in a choir is unique in its glory. God's breath, His *ruach*, collectively enters the lungs of immortal souls, and what is exhaled is glorious worship.

The world of orchestral music where harmonic color can express truth without the help of words, was a revelation for me in high school. In "Fantasia on a Theme" by Thomas Tallis, English composer Ralph Vaughan Williams took a setting of Psalm 2 and expanded it into an aural cathedral for the mind and spirit. I will never forget my first experience of the work at age seventeen—I felt like I had been struck by lightning—every nerve raw, all my emotions converted to tears. To this day, I have encountered the Holy Spirit innumerable times through those particular colors and chords, witnessing glimpses of truth and beauty even before I had a framework for understanding that I was hearing the echoes of God's beauty.

•••

I chased *Sehnsucht* in the unseen to study the Renaissance for a semester in Italy, all the way through a graduate degree in classical music, and through the confusion of becoming a young adult in a sea of ideologies and insecurities. I did not grow up with a deep theological understanding of the world, or with a perception of a God who cultivates a longing in us that will not be satisfied with any artifact of the world. I didn't meet this God until I was twenty-five or so, the fruit of a season where my patient friend Laura took the time to untangle my doubts and fears about faith with me in friendship. In her witness, one of the most compelling arguments I heard on the path to seeing the God-in-flesh, the one who satisfies all debts and longings, was that this *Sehnsucht* was created by God and could finally be satisfied in Jesus. This was a kind of hope I had never come across.

You see, even as a teenager, I learned the sunsets would not last on the Loess Hills. I spent my allowance trying to capture them on film. Roll after roll shot and submitted to the lab, I was always alight with anticipation when I picked up my film. But all that was left, as beautiful as the shot might have come out, was a shadow of what the experience had been. Vanity of vanities! I could never really grasp the beauty. Such is the fleeting nature of art-making too. I could finish a painting but the vision had only been translated in part. I could perform a song cycle, but the experience was transient and there was always silence on the other end of the performance, long after the audience left. For here we have no continuing city. After all of these experiences, the door to the longing still stood lonely and open, waiting for a permanent resident in the mansion of my soul. The art itself had become unsatisfying, even bitter at times, because it couldn't deliver what it seemed to promise.

There is a reason that C.S. Lewis calls the sensation of *Sehnsucht* "an inconsolable secret." It is inconsolable, except perhaps on the other side of what Shakespeare's *Macbeth* calls this bank and shoal of time. The scriptures say that when we die, we'll be united with eternity himself, reconciled to the beauty and home we so long for through the cross of Christ, or we will be left wandering, eternally homesick. We either embrace or reject the notion that what we do and believe here, on this bank and shoal of time, matters. This place is not eternity, and neither is the art we produce under the sun. Mortal life exists in the shallows, and God's eternity flows all around this shoal, from beginning to end. What we do on the shoal determines which current catches us in the ocean of eternity.

•••

Beauty is cruel if all it does is tear us open and lay us bare, leaving us vulnerable to the changing tides of the world, thirsty and drowning. When I began to realize what *Sehnsucht* really was, it was like watching my entire life come into focus. Everything suddenly made sense. The idea that the greatest symphony, painting, work of literature or poetry, or fearsome display of nature are all artifacts whose beauty only marginally reflect the true nature and person of the triune God is one that is profound in its truth. All the beautiful artifacts of the world will not outlast the immortal human soul, or the God whose image we bear. All my longing to know and understand art pales in comparison to my desire to know and understand the God of my longing through His word.

In the same way that Schiller's words, "Even beauty must perish," are immortalized in my aural memory through the music of Brahms, so are the words of Isaiah 40:6-8. "All flesh is as grass, and all its beauty is like the flower of the field. The grass withers, the flower fades...but the word of God will stand forevermore." Meditation on the word of God pushes that door in me a little more open each time I partake, and the feast it promises is everlasting. When this meditation is amplified by art, my experience of God is only more intense.

For now, I can reasonably expect the experience of *Sehnsucht* as a part of creaturely life, walking upon a shoal, forward, forward, from birth toward death. We occasionally step into one of those grooves where the current has carved a shape, like the Sehnsucht carves a landscape in us. The current is not imaginary, although we cannot see it. We feel the pull, though we don't always notice the slow shaping. The landscape of the human heart is constantly being formed by our senses, habits, and our nursing of secret desire. We may resist or lean into the current, and even get swept away in it for a time.

In Ecclesiastes 3:11, Qoheleth says that God has "put eternity into man's heart, yet so that he cannot find out what God has done from the beginning to the end." This is a gift, this longing, and so too is the inability to discover the perfect fulfillment of it here on earth. This gift is from a God who wants not to confound us with riddles, but who wishes to draw us to Him. He has embedded the secret of *Sehnsucht* within us to carve out a space for Himself, and then He reveals Himself to us through His word and through the presence of the Holy Spirit, carving the channels in our heart ever deeper. He gives us Himself, the only fulfillment of *Sehnsucht,* in a relational way, in a way that grows with time and intimacy. This intimacy culminates in an everlasting marriage in the eternal depths of God's beauty and love, where no veil will separate us from Him. Instead of standing in the shallows of His beauty, we will be soaked in the depths of it forever, home at last.

Kelly Kruse

Writer & Artist

OUR HEARTS IN INK

Sean O'Hare

I HAVE ALWAYS ENVIED those people who, from the time of their twelfth birthday, have their entire career trajectory mapped out. The confidence with which they lay out their watertight plan to become a veterinarian or dentist always left me profoundly acquainted with the aimlessness of my own life goals.

It produced something akin to the experience of reading a biography of some great historical figure, against whose towering achievements one always feels equal parts inspired and dejected.

Unsurprisingly, the effects of my own personal career drift was a period of about six months after my high school graduation, during which I sat brooding at home, with neither a collegiate plan or a job. The—also inevitable—outcome of this was an uncomfortable conversation with my parents, when they informed me, lovingly, gently, of course, that I needed to find myself some work. So I applied for positions and found a part time job that would pay me to crawl out of bed in the middle of the night and work until the sun came up.

EXHAUSTED IN THE WAREHOUSE

There I labored in a warehouse full of boxes. Endless piles of them. The tangle of chutes and belts in that place was like the circulatory system of some lumbering, clumsy giant, pushing boxes through clogged passageways, always pouring more out onto the belts where the trucks were parked. My task was to unload the docked trailers, fresh off the highway that hummed just a half mile from the warehouse, trailers that came from Kansas and Montana and California with unending stacks of those dreadful brown packages.

It was in one of those cold, dark trailers in the middle of the night that I gained my first glimpse of clarity. Here I was, less than a week into my new line of work and already I found myself utterly exhausted, still in those terrible stages where the body, before it is benumbed altogether, rebels against the awful conditions pressed upon it in places like that warehouse.

That night in the trailer, as I saw a life for myself surrounded by an infinite sea of nothing but boxes, I resolved that I would not stay there, that I could not stay there. I would go to college and find a different way to make my living. Not because I was better than these people I worked alongside—for whom I had already gained an immense respect—but because I simply yearned for something fundamentally different, something outside the universe of this warehouse. I did not know it then, but it was stories that I longed for: ancient texts, modern translations, ideas and philosophies and histories. That great conversation which has been unfolding for millennia began to hound me, showing itself to me in snatches, drawing me further in.

•••

And so I went to school. A few months later I found myself at the local community college, my intellectual home for the next year and a half. I remained uncertain of which bachelor's degree I wanted to pursue, so I took general courses, emerging on the other end with an Associate's degree in Liberal Arts. A good start, I told myself. I did well enough in those courses, read enough of the chapters and articles to satisfy my teachers, did enough of the exercises and homework assignments to graduate with a respectable GPA. Something was awakened here, but not fully; a foundation laid for further scaffolding.

The blue-collar work continued apace. While attending school, I landscaped and delivered pizzas. After graduation I was hired by a moving company to work as a diesel mechanic in their shop, changing tires and drum brakes and rebuilding engines. Somewhere in the middle of all this I found myself reading more and more in my free time. I don't know how it began, nor can I account for its growth, but soon it consumed me, filling every free moment. The Gojo soap never cleaned out all the grit, so I went to lunch with dirty hands, oil-soaked shirts and Lewis's *Mere Christianity* tucked under my arm.

THE READING CONSUMES

I read of Dietrich Bonhoeffer's life, listened on my morning commute to historical novels I had checked out from the library. An intricate dance began to emerge between these two threads of my life: working in a world of trucks, wrenches and oil; reading of philosophy, theology, and history. The questions of life presented themselves to me through the real, entrenched features of my everyday experiences, and were answered and posed again in ink.

The fiction I read was no fiction at all. When I looked up from the page, I saw deeper into the text. When I looked back at the page, the whole world inhabited it anew, filling it again with the colors and characters that animated life with such jarring vibrancy, such unrelenting personality and energy.

As this bookish dance continued, I began to see that this was in fact no new development but a fresh manifestation of something I had already been given, growing from the literary and intellectual tradition I had received in middle and high school.

I was homeschooled my whole life, and both parents had planted a love for literature deep in my heart. Our family often read books together in the evening; we belligerently debated ideas, passages, and politics over dinner and then long after dinner had ended. Whole days spent in the local library were a common occurrence, and we listened incessantly to dramatized productions of the *Chronicles of Narnia* and *Les Misérables*. Notably, a central feature of my homeschool education was the development of an ability to select new pathways of learning, interrogating ideas as directed by my interests and under the steady guidance of my mother.

These habits lay dormant for a time, but slowly awakened after my college years. Now I was free to pursue whatever interested me, having been equipped to take it up. And there was little that did not interest me. This of course presented a glorious dilemma: there were far too many books to be read. In fact, I soon began to realize that there really was no such thing as a singular book, that the concept of a distinct piece of literature truly is a tenuous claim. In reality, I began to see that the boundaries of a book were merely a thin film through which countless other texts—which themselves contained a myriad of others—bled in and out.

Each book was unique only in the sense that it was able to synthesize its predecessors in its own peculiar manner. Beyond this, to speak of a book as existing within a vacuum was a failure to perceive the thousands of minds at work within its pages; to read one book was to read a dozen others, was to read its influences and its antithesis. In the same way I could not untangle books from the world around me, I could not untangle them from each other. They were inextricably bound to their counterparts through some mysterious force I did not fully understand.

To this project I turned with a passion, seeking out the sources of each text that I had stumbled upon, straining to hear the voices reverberating throughout their pages. I read Chesterton and he spoke of Dickens with a kind of awe; I read Dickens, and in his tales I saw the very same faces that pulled the trucks behind the shop for me to work on, the faces that had filled the warehouse I worked in years before. I discovered *The Iliad*'s influence on the Western canon, so I read of Hector and Achilles and the great quarrel of their people. I consumed Tolkien's trilogy and was drawn into the ancient world he had wrought; soon I was exploring its annals further, reading of Beren and Luthien in *The Silmarillion.* I read in one book a passage taken from Tolstoy's *Confessions;* I went to it and found the same spiritual and philosophical questions which had filled my own mind since youth, gathered into a single narrative and articulated with an unparalleled clarity and power; because of this I turned to *Anna Karenina,* read of jealousy and forgiveness and despair, of Levin's struggles within himself and with the ultimate questions of existence.

AN INSATIABLE HUNGER FOR WORDS

My insatiable hunger for words soon drove me to seek a deeper knowledge of that intermediary, translating element: the mind of a writer. How was it that one could bring the literary and physical worlds together in such a way as to produce a truer version of each one? With every new book I began to observe how different authors, old and new, accomplished this in their own unique way. Eventually, because I had been setting down roots within literary soil for so long, a desire to try my own hand at the craft began to grow.

I can recall distinctly the experience of reading Chesterton for the first time, of loving it so much that I foolishly suspected I could write something just like it—or at least close to it. So I tried to write like Chesterton. And I failed of course; not because I didn't know the streets of London well enough to make witty analogies of them, but because I lacked the gargantuan, expansive mind, the spiritual maturity, the biting wit, the unbridled vitality and energy that crouched behind every syllable. I had not lived the life of Chesterton, had not read the books he had read, was unable to truly emulate his style for the simple fact that his style had run its course with the last word that he had penned. And mine, I soon began to see, was taking its own shape, taking a piece of his style, to be sure, but was forming itself to the contours of my own life. It was being filled with my unique memories and images, the particular books I had read, the people I had spoken to. So I kept on writing, learning what I could from teachers like Austen, Poe, Longfellow, Dostoyevsky, Wordsworth, and Hugo, practicing the craft as often as I could.

Enter the Internet. As my literary horizons expanded, so too did the possibilities in this arena. I found so many others on blogs and journals and forums who had been at this for much longer, who were reading with a sharper analytical eye, who were writing with more clarity and carrying out intricate conversations on complex questions. I soon developed an affinity for the sprawling style of *New Yorker* profiles, devoured book reviews wherever they could be found, followed bloggers and online writers as they carried out far-ranging debates. These online connections even spilled over into the real world. One spring, I drove down to South Carolina and attended a week-long ethics and philosophy course led by a theologian and writer whose blog I had been reading for years.

In so many online spaces I found that the nature of discourse was particularly suited for robust conversations playing out in real time, essays that begot essays that begot more essays. Here was the opportunity to peer into the world of academia and scholarship, to perceive some of its intricacies and the personalities that populated it. All this in turn greatly sharpened my own ideas, introducing me to a world I had never thought existed, that I found myself wishing I could be a part of. And so I read on and wrote more, and found places that would publish my work, and eventually a place that entrusted to me the task of publishing and curating the writing of others.

More years passed.

THE DREAM OF CAMBRIDGE

On a bright spring day in 2019 I found myself on a double-decker bus, approaching the city of Cambridge from the English countryside. On the ride into the city, I reflected on the vocational drift that still hounded me years after my graduation from community college. Although I was still reading and writing voraciously on my own time, I remained no closer to a vision for my life's work. To add to the sting, only a few months prior I had dropped out of a calculus class.

Since my time as a diesel mechanic I had spent the past few years working as a technician at a scientific research facility in my city. There I gathered data for scientists who came from all over the world to conduct bizarre, fascinating physics experiments.

The university that ran the lab offered excellent tuition benefits for a STEM-related degree, prompting me to eventually sign up for mathematics courses. I labored through them, but it soon became clear to me that I had no special affinity for numbers. Finally, after a few semesters of this mirage, the calculus class was dropped and hopes of an engineering career were abandoned. This produced in me a growing confusion and frustration. I was unable to determine a clear path to follow from there and increasingly uncertain about what the future held.

It was against this backdrop that I traveled for two weeks in Europe at the generous invitation of my uncle. The final leg of my trip found me in an English town a few miles outside of Cambridge, staying with friends who encouraged me to spend a day exploring the nearby city.

The bus was stopping now and I went along on foot into the city, passing Magdalene College where C.S. Lewis had taught medieval literature, then up and over the bridge that spans the River Cam. I heard the punters call to each other with mirth in their voices as they meandered by me on the winding river. More colleges were on my right now, their ancient buildings rising proudly against the brilliant spring sky. Students rolled by me on their bikes, porters guarded the college entrances against curious tourists like myself, and professors emerged from old stone buildings and hurried along on foot with their work tucked under their arm.

With each step I felt a growing sense of clarity. I wandered down side streets and past towering churches, passed the college grounds where Newton had walked, found Lewis's favorite pub where he had spent so many hours with Tolkien. From the top of Great St. Mary's church I looked out over the town, taking in the colleges where Wordsworth and Darwin and Hawking had studied. Across the street was the magnificent King's College Chapel. There I was overtaken with awe at the stunning vaulted ceilings and the intricate scenes in stained glass that lined the hall, the brilliant afternoon sunlight slanting through the panes and filling the chapel with a thousand colored rays.

Later that afternoon I crossed Parker's Piece, an open, grassy park, so caught up with excitement that I entertained searching for an office where I could inquire about an application. I was a tourist there that day, yet I could not stop imagining myself as a student, walking those same streets with a new kind of purpose. I had never been able to picture anything more vividly than this.

I felt the uncertainty of the past few months and years melt away completely. Here it seemed that my reading had not been a random string of books, but a coherent pattern that mapped so well onto this storied institution. And although I had longed in recent years for a life that centered around reading and scholarship, it had taken the act of standing here surrounded by all these ancient colleges of learning for me to put that yearning into words.

Back at the house, I told my friends of my remarkable day and deluded scheming. Instead of laughter I was greeted with enthusiasm. That very night, I decided I would apply to the University of Cambridge to study English Literature.

The following months brought endless paperwork. Personal statements, an academic reference from the theologian I had studied with, digging up old school records for my application. Friends and family offered support, some came to my aid with their invaluable expertise. Finally, after submitting my application, I received a request for written work; a few weeks later, an invitation for an interview. I traveled to Cambridge for the interview, then back home again. I waited.

And then there it was.

"I am delighted to inform you..."

An email from my college, telling me that I would be spending the next three years in Cambridge reading English Literature. The past eight years of wandering, failing, working, reading, and writing all finally captured and answered in a single sentence.

"We would like to make you an offer..."

My mind rushed back to those disheartening six months at home after high school, the jobs shoveling mulch and changing tires and gathering scientific data. I was deeply grateful for all of it—not in some romantic sense, but because of the real experiences and wisdom it had imparted to me. I felt again what it had been like surrounded by boxes on that night in the frigid trailer, a still unformed vision seizing me in that moment.

If only I had known what it would bring. I recalled how that had prompted my return to school, picking up books again, the headlong rush that followed, the years trying my own hand at the craft of writing, the countless conversations with family and friends about the books we read and what they meant to our lives.

And in this slow unfolding of my own tale, I see too that heaving multitude of human minds which came before, those mighty souls who knew that to write down the mysteries of this life is to see them more clearly; that to read them back again is to know oneself and the world that ever presses in upon us. Day rolls into day, and year to year, and still we spill our hearts in ink, and find ourselves reflected on the page.

Sean O'Hare
Writer & Academic

ON QUESTIONS & ANSWERS

Jane Zwart

Q. What is your only comfort in life and in death?

A. That I am not my own, but belong with body and soul, both in life and in death, to my faithful Saviour Jesus Christ. He has fully paid for all my sins with his precious blood, and has set me free from all the power of the devil. He also preserves me in such a way that without the will of my heavenly Father not a hair can fall from my head; indeed, all things must work together for my salvation. Therefore, by his Holy Spirit he also assures me of eternal life and make me heartily willing and ready from now on to live for him.

Lord's Day 1, *Heidelberg Catechism*

Be patient toward all that is unsolved in your heart and try to love the questions themselves, like locked rooms and like books that are now written in a very foreign tongue. Do not now seek the answers, which cannot be given you because you would not be able to live them. And the point is, to live everything. Live the questions now. Perhaps you will then gradually, without noticing it, live along some distant day into the answer.

Rainer Maria Rilke, *Letters to a Young Poet*

TWO DECADES AGO, when I was a student at Calvin College, I fell in love with Rainer Maria Rilke. Smitten with *Letters to a Young Poet* and enamoured, too, with the notion that I was a young poet, I painstakingly copied Rilke's injunction to "love the questions themselves." Copying things painstakingly was my wont back then. Back then, I thought that anguish was poetic. I smirked at what had sheltered me. And I mistook spurning answers for loving the questions themselves.

Such overreactions are a staple of the bildungsroman. In adolescence, many of us demote our parents from omnipotence to folly for slender cause. We swap asperity for niceties, and repeatedly epiphanies dawn on us as if they were exactly what the teacher in Ecclesiastes says don't exist: new things under the sun. And that's the mild strain of the developmental stage—the version of adolescence that time is dialectic enough to cure, such that eventually one's parents come into focus as the thoughtful, fallible people they always were and honesty no longer seems to require the blunt utterance of every truth and new realizations do not demand the toppling and recreating of worlds.

An adolescent at 18, I came down with the usual symptoms. That is, I didn't just fall in with Rainer Maria Rilke. I didn't just careen into love of the questions themselves. No, I also fell in line with *A Catcher in the Rye*'s Holden Caulfield and *Winesburg, Ohio*'s George Willard. I made it a point of pride that I could match them for disillusionment, not recognizing that I also matched them for illusions. I fell in line with *Mrs. Dalloway*'s Sally Seton, too. She beheaded "all sorts of flowers that had never been seen together" and floated them in bowls, dismaying old ladies;[1] I carried out the vivisection of my art history textbook and tucked a knobby, naked Egon Schiele and a leery Cindy Sherman into my wallet, appalling my wholesome college dorm resident advisor. I flattered myself that Sally Seton

---

1   Virginia Woolf, *Mrs. Dalloway* (1925).

and I had this in common: both of us knew better than to trust any art that hid what beauty costs. I read these characters as interrogating everything, and I set out to plot my own story after theirs.

Now that I teach these books, though, I notice things that I missed back then. For one, I notice *Winesburg, Ohio*'s last sentence, where George Willard regards his childhood town as "but a background on which to paint the dreams of his manhood."[2] As a first-year student, I sighed at that line with uncritical fellow-feeling. Now, I pick up on the wry ambiguity in the phrase "the dreams of his manhood." Is George's manhood itself a dream, or is it sturdy enough to have a brood of dreams that belong to it? Likewise, I revisit that ambiguous construct I was trying to press my childhood into the background for: the weight of loving the questions. Did loving the questions constitute a burden, or did loving the questions carry weight?

The answer, for me, was both. Loving the questions did, sometimes, solidify into an object, its heft approximately that of a household idol. At other times, loving the questions allowed me to exact the weight of suffering more honestly than I could have otherwise. I believe the weight of loving the questions amounts to both those realities for a fair number of Calvin's undergrads these days, too.

Which is why, looking back at my first, flagrant love for the questions themselves, I find myself tempted to generalize, claiming that my current students resemble my 18-year-old self. After all, that claim could ground the case I'd like to make for empathy as crucial to my efforts in the classroom. And that case does have its merits. Empathy does often take hold of me when I teach.

For instance, every time that I assign a core literature class excerpts from the first three books of *Gulliver's Travels*, I warm

---

2   Sherwood Anderson, *Winesburg, Ohio* (1919).

to the students who warm to Swift's satire, interrogating his narrator, Gulliver, who is every bit as naïve as his name advertises. I resonate with these students' inquiries because I've questioned the text in much the same spirit (i.e., with a woe that is three-quarters amusement). I find their laughter contagious because I've cackled over the same scenes.

Take Gulliver's tour of an island where pompous intellectuals perform impractical—indeed, purposeless—experiments. He counts these eggheads great prodigies, whereas those of us whom Swift has in stitches have a long enough acquaintance with such posturers, such professors not to be overawed. In its earliest stages, then, my empathy with these students might draw on nothing more than shared mirth, or, to put a finer point on it, self-congratulatory camaraderie. We chuckle together because Gulliver questions nothing, and because we would interrogate all of it: the Lilliputians' tidy provincialism and the Brobdingnagians' crass hospitality, not to mention the scholar, head in clouds, smelling of the excrement he intends to convert back into food, but equally ripe with vanity.

Collective smugness is not, however, empathy at its best, which is why I would not bother assigning *Gulliver's Travels* were it not for its fourth book, which numbers among literature's great chastening fictions. In Book Four, Gulliver apprentices himself to a race of horses whose whole calculus is reason. And from this utterly disinterested species, he learns cynicism, forswearing his earlier wonderment at human things. On his eventual return to England, in fact, he classes his wife, his children, and his neighbours as mere "Yahoos," aspiring only to find them tolerable. Indeed, Gulliver has moved from incredulity without discernment to incredulity without charity. He loves only the questions now.

Well, by this time, my students have quit laughing, and I know, from experience, that some of them are indicting themselves for having been as disdainful as this caricature of Swift's.

Some of them are sounding themselves for the habit of merciless inquisition, some even for the idolatry of loving only the questions (which *Gulliver's Travels* hints is a greater transgression even than the unquestioning adoration for silly things). I warm to them at this juncture, too. After all, I've arraigned myself over the same wrongs, and in part thanks to this same book. And that commonality between us permits me to teach from a place of empathy.

So I tell my students what *Gulliver's Travels* has taught me. Reading this fiction, I say, helped me to understand that cynicism isn't the opposite of naïveté. It is, in fact, a form of naïveté—but one we're a little quicker to find attractive than goofy credulity is, because this version comes with an angsty sense of superiority attached. But that sense of superiority is still folly, at bottom, and it moves a cynical Gulliver, for instance, to assume that any question he cannot answer must not have an answer; consequently, he can see no further than the worth of his questions. To be fair, he does pose some worthy questions. Gulliver asks why, when they make us so backward, we love our vices. He asks, more broadly, what justifies the irrationality of love. And, in truth, Gulliver's problem is not that he cannot answer these queries. The problem is that he takes the limits of what he can fathom as absolute. I think we do the same thing in our own moments or seasons of cynicism, I conclude, and I think when we assume the questions we cannot answer have no answers, we are already courting idolatry—for by then we've ruled out the mind of God, the heart of God.

I'm willing to admit that teaching *Gulliver's Travels*—and probably a good many other texts—I can pivot into the mode of the sermon, even into confession. But that is what teaching from a place of empathy requires of me: seeing the provisions that a student needs because you've had to collect the same equipment and, in turn, lending them what you have ready to hand. And to equip my students with such truths, to reach them via empathy, is a great part of my vocation.

Even so, the truth is that my empathy for these students who feel a bit like kin—it's not enough. Empathy does, after all, hinge on familiarity, and only sometimes am I able to trace the kinship between my story and my students' stories. Indeed, for every student overreacting to their upbringing in the direction of idolizing the questions, as I once did, is another who fears the questions. Which means that to rely solely on empathy as a means of reaching my students is less than my vocation requires. Put otherwise: to depend just on empathy in the classroom would be to generalize, to teach from a false premise.

Part of my vocation, then, has been learning a wider compassion—compassion, for instance, for the student who bristled on reading Emily Dickinson's poem "This World is not Conclusion." The lines she objected to were these:

"Faith slips — and laughs, and rallies
    — Blushes, if any see —

Plucks at a twig of Evidence
    — And asks a Vane, the way —"

Now, admittedly, part of the trouble stemmed from a misreading of the poem. My student took these lines as pointing to an infirm faith (it slips), a less than serious faith (it laughs when it slips), a faith embarrassed of itself (it blushes). My empathy never balks at a student's misreading of a poem, though; I know I've done the same. Still, I cannot empathize with an experience of faith exempt from slipping. Doubt has, at times, left me far from surefooted, and I've also crossed at least one stretch of icy nonchalance. Nor can I empathize with a faith that has no laughter in it.

Finding myself unable to conjure up empathy for this student's experience of faith, however, does not mean that I cannot, by the grace of God, summon compassion for her. And I did. I pointed her, gently, to the word "rallies" in the poem, and asked her what she thought it meant. "Does it mean Faith gets its balance back?" she ventured. "I think it does," I said, and then I asked, "And if it gets its balance back, then what is it blushing about?" She paused. "Its clumsiness," she answered. And from there, I could go on.

I could grant that different varieties of clumsiness enter into our experiences of faith.

More importantly still, I could point to the fact that the poem suggests that whatever our particular clumsiness, there are provisions enough and providence enough to let us rally, to give us our balance back.

But Dickinson calls those provisions a "twig of Evidence" and "a Vane," and I couldn't help noticing that as I read out the next two lines, this student who objected to an infirm faith reknit her brow. "I bet," I said, "some of us don't like the idea that it's only a 'twig of Evidence.' Why not a whole branch? Why not a whole tree? A whole forest?" The young woman nodded vigorously. And another student piped up, "Is that 'Vane' a weather vane?" "It is," I said, and he suggested that this is a problem, too, since a weather vane turns at the wind's whim, meaning that it has none of the steady guidance of, say, a compass, which is, he asserted, what we need in our faith.

"Right," I replied. "So if we read this line about the weather vane as arguing there's no clear route to God's presence or the line about the twig as claiming there's not much evidence for God's existence, those of us who are Christians have good reason to dispute this poem. But I suspect," I continued, "that what Dickinson wants us to realize is that the world is so full of God's glory that even a twig—not only a twig, even a twig—testifies to his creativity. As for the weather vane, you're right that it's not reliable if you're using it in place of a compass, if you know what direction to go already. But I think that the poem is making the point that even if you come with more questions than anything else, God's providence is enough that you could strike out in any direction and find him. So it's not that there's no clear route into God's presence; it's that there's every clear route to his presence. And I do love that," I say.

Maybe these two students (and a fair number of others) still don't exit the classroom loving these lines. Maybe, too, we—they and I—have halted, in understanding each other, some distance from empathy. But maybe, maybe Dickinson's little allegory of clumsy Faith, long on questions, will come back to these students when they need it. I hope so.

Indeed, I hope I have lent them, no less than the students for whom I find ready empathy, some equipage for living in the contested space between questions and answers. Because every semester I watch my students navigating this very space, checking the cords that bind them to Christian belief, sometimes to test their slack and sometimes to be sure of their knots. And here is what I want to tell them: Dear people, "Be patient toward all that is unsolved in your heart and try to love the questions." Be patient and love the questions, I want to tell them, because it is an answer we live inevitably exceeds any words we try to fit to it.

Jane Zwart
Professor & Co-Director
Calvin Center for Faith & Writing

SWEETNESS FOLLOWS

Sara Billups

WE'RE DEVELOPMENTALLY HARD-WIRED to blend in when we're young, probably to survive the universal drag of middle school. I wanted to disappear in the bleachers throughout adolescence. Then, the magic grasp of conformity slipped. This waking up from a pre-teen hibernation happened the same time I started freshman year, when I was also the new kid.

At the new school, it took a little while. I started buying vintage dresses at the Dove's Nest thrift shop my freshman year, before I'd met any students at the Lutheran high school. That fall, I scanned the weekly chapel service to identify the kids who would become my friends by searching for visual cues: Dr. Martens, Manic Panic hair dye, or granny cardigan sweaters. It would be a little while before my first kiss with the boy I saw playing guitar under an oversized Martin Luther statue at the local seminary, or our walks by the night lake.

It would be a little while longer before I would first see my now husband in the dining commons of our Christian college, wearing a baseball hat that said "Automatic for the People." He bought it at the BBQ restaurant in Athens, Georgia, with a tagline that inspired the name of the album I'd played so many times it had melted into my mind—taffy to shag carpet.

Somewhere in between the first boy and the last, I bought a golden yellow cassette at Target and played it, on repeat, for years: R.E.M.'s 1993 album *Automatic for the People*. I didn't know any Christians who wrote jungle-thick dreamscapes of lyrics like the band's singer Michael Stipe, even though I kept looking.

•••

I am an orphaned believer. Like many of my Gen X and Millennial peers, I have experienced a spiritual and cultural orphaning. I'm a person of faith who has encountered a certain creative alienation from suburban church culture. As a Christian, I've also been orphaned in broader culture, where following Jesus costs social capital and does little for personal brand.

My obsession with *Automatic for the People* was a first articulation of a high school-aged orphaned believer. The album toggled between counterculture and dominant culture. *Automatic* was ubiquitous in the early '90s, and on heavy radio rotation.

Lots of us listened to *Automatic*, Christians and non-Christians and everyone else I knew. My friends and I were territorial because it was our very own album. We were the ones getting together on Friday nights to listen together and pick apart lyrics. But we knew full well that the jock, geek, and youthiest of youth group kids knew all the lines to "Everybody Hurts," too. Album lyrics like "I will see things that you'll never see" and "I have got to leave to find my way" tapped into my own teenage identity. Often busy dreaming the classic dream—leaving my small town for the city—*Automatic* was a backdrop for an emerging imagination.

I once listened to the album in the car with my school's pom pom team captain. "You know how someone is a real friend?" the pom pom captain asked me between verses. "When you don't have to say anything and feel totally comfortable." The moment felt important, like a movie.

Automatic was an escape from our midwestern cultural and spiritual orphaning. We were escape artists while listening. We were not wearing dance squad ribbons and high ponytails. We were not driving to the basketball game to perform "Eye of the Tiger" on the high gloss floor. I was riding shotgun, and we were Indiana happy-sad, and nobody needed to say anything.

In our church by the strip mall, no one appeared particularly sad or happy. We were present. You could have called roll and the same families would be perched in the same pew every week. "Present." Tracing my finger over the notes in the hymnal, I was in my own body and estranged from it.

I thought of the lake at the seminary, and its chapel and the first boy. Built in the 1950s by a famous Finnish architect, the seminary chapel looks like two playing cards gingerly stacked to form a steep triangular roofline. There are 168 triangles covering the rear sanctuary wall, each equaling an hour and adding up to a week's worth of hours. The roofline casts a triangular shelter in my mind, a triune God hovering over the water.

•••

The Anchor Room, our town's Christian bookstore, reserved a small section in the back for Tooth and Nail bands. I bought CDs from the record label with names like Luxury, Starflyer 59, and Blenderhead. I learned that this label was based in Seattle, and that's all I needed to know to decide: the Pacific Northwest was a mythic mountain of Christian counterculture, and I was going to live there someday.

But not until I finished high school and undergrad in Indiana. For a lot of years, the closest I could get to seeing many of these Tooth and Nail bands was at a midwestern music festival in rural Illinois, which I attended for a string of summers in the late '90s and early aughts.

Buses full of youth group kids and old Jesus People gathered together on a farm for a week, and for five days each summer my faith life and my creative leanings clicked into place. Here, I found other Christians interested in the same books, artists, and music I was, and it was immensely liberating.

At the lake on the music festival grounds, we swam and washed our candy color-dyed hair. We listened to bands play from lunchtime till midnight. In between performances, I walked around the campsites and food tents with the teenaged feeling that more is ahead than behind. Now in my 40s, I've begun to pray Psalm 90:15: "Make us glad for as many days as you have afflicted us, for as many years as we have seen trouble."

•••

I wrote a list of the Christians who shaped my faith during my teens and twenties. My own mother. The chaplain who carved mini wooden crosses on strings for each student in our school that I still keep hung around my headboard. Next to it, I wrote a list of the musicians, artists, and writers who shaped my aesthetic. Patti Smith, Jean-Michel Basquiat, and Annie Dillard.

In her apocalyptic 1982 essay "Total Eclipse" on watching a solar eclipse near Yakima, Washington, Dillard writes: "We teach our children one thing only, as we were taught: to wake up.... We live half our waking lives and all of our sleeping lives in some private, useless and insensible waters we never mention or recall. Useless, I say."

I held an index card with a tiny hole poked in the middle up to the sky during a solar eclipse in 1994, standing with my friends on a hill next to the high school. We were displaced together, but really awake, as the moon floated between the earth and the sun. I wondered if I would melt my eye if I took the card away for too long, and tried it. Sun spots.

"Valueless, I might add—until someone hauls their wealth up to the surface and into the wide-awake city," Dillard continues, "in a form that people can use." I thought often in those years about Patti Smith and Basquiat in New York City. Their work was brave and wholly itself, rising far above my weekends browsing CDs at the chain CD store in the mall.

I wish the lists of my spiritual formation and creative formation crossed over more than they do. I did not grow up with a Christian imagination. In my family, we did not talk about mystery. We were in the throes of the culture wars, and my father talked about Tipper Gore's "Parental Guidance: Explicit Lyrics" stickers on CDs and Robert Mapplethorpe's scandalous art.

I came of age in a cultural moment flanked by apologetics, rational propositions and arguments to counter secular postmodernism. Back then, Dad thought we could argue other people into the kingdom. My family talked about theological positions so much that we left no room for healthy doubt, faith and art, or lament.

The church's focus on culture wars cultivated a sort of defensiveness in my family that allowed for little faith-based creative exploration. When we're in a fight or flight posture, it is less likely we can access a prolific sense of wonder and imagination.

•••

I listened to *Automatic* with my son on a recent drive. He's now a few years younger than I was when I first heard the album. I asked him how the music made him feel. "Melancholy, but restful." Listening to lyrics like "sweetness follows," I like to think he picked up on some sense of mystery, and the way God created music, and that music is a good gift.

I want there to be room for him to be a part of the global church that lifts up our thinking minds and celebrates our creative minds. I want him to find Christian artists creating more weird, surprising, and imaginative writing, music, and art in church communities. Where those of us who have experienced a cultural orphaning can find a home for more than a long weekend at a music festival.

He'll probably find his way through his own particular orphaning with help from his own favorite band. And maybe the church can be cool water when he is thirsty. And a night lake when he is lamenting. And a bright light he moves toward, and not away from.

Sara Billups
Writer & Podcaster

ON UNNECESSARILY OWNING ART

Karen Stiller

LAST SEPTEMBER, I floated in a COVID-fog through Fredericton's Gallery on Queen Street with our oldest son. Our moods matched the drizzle outside. We were, all of us, still startled to be wandering through a pandemic. Logging the disappointments and losses was an almost daily activity in the early days of that fall.

This was not supposed to happen. That was supposed to happen. I am not supposed to be here. We were supposed to be there. On some days, it was hard not to take the pandemic personally.

My biggest lament, back then, was releasing my first memoir during those uncertain days. "Stop your whining and just be grateful," my inner shusher shushed. But I had fantasized of success—I admit it. I could close my eyes and see my book's name up in lights. It feels silly now, and embarrassing to confess. But some hope of "making it" is part of any maker's making, right? Otherwise, how would we ever finish anything? Where would we find the gall to push things out into the world that had not requested one single thing from us?

On that day, I walked through the gallery in gloom. When I came eye to eye with a small 12x12 inch painting called "Becoming" by Amy Ash, I cried. It was mixed media on wood, sturdy to hold, soft in color. Seven women stand sketched in a loose knot, talking. They look like women of a certain era, by the pouf of their hair, their sensible shoes, the length of a skirt and their solidity. They are women who know things—the neighbor ladies with the answers we needed, or a band-aid.

I looked, the tears came and I was comforted. By then, I had heard from a few readers who, through the magic of memoir, had read themselves into my book. I was deeply grateful. The crowds that my giant-tiny ego had dreamt of had shrunk down to a small intimate group of readers who felt like new friends—and there they were in a circle, standing in the art right in front of me.

That's why I cried. I bought the painting almost immediately. In my living room now, the piece still reassures me with its message that small can be strong. I've lifted it right off the wall and held it up to zoom calls, to show people. "This," I say. "This is how I try to see things now."

•••

"Artists are the conduits of life, articulating what all of us are sensing, but may not have the capacity to express," writes Makoto Fujimura in his wonderful book, *Art + Faith: A Theology of Making.*

My husband and I purchased our first "articulation of what we were sensing" back at Regent College in the '90s, from what was then called The Lookout Gallery. Brent was a seminary student and I was a hard worker. We often ran out of money, but that was all part of it. We frequented a restaurant that offered endless french fry refills. We'd sit there for an hour shamelessly eating fries off one shared plate until we could eat no more, wondering if the waitress would scold us.

I asked my husband this morning if he remembered what we paid for the watercolor hanging in our kitchen. It is a painting of two hands, bold against a bright blue background, passing a yellow coffee cup between them. "...more coffee?" is penciled at the bottom. And then: "Oh yes!" Brent answered immediately: "Ninety dollars."

That would have been a lot for us. We would have thought about that, and weighed the cost against some bill. There would have been more prudent ways to spend what would have been hard-earned. Always, that is true. Probably one of us felt more certain that buying art was a good idea, and nudged the other one forward. And then there would have been a shot of pleasure at making a married-couple-purchase that was not mixing bowls or winter tires or milk and eggs, but instead something made by hand and so pleasingly composed and rendered, joyful with color and meaning. Valuable just for being beautiful. Here was something to hang up and hang onto, throughout all these years.

I still remember what that piece articulated for us back then, just starting out. We wanted to be people who practiced hospitality. "More coffee?" "Oh yes!" That was just the start of it.

•••

When we left our first parish postings in northern Saskatchewan, the two churches Brent served banded together and gave us an envelope that contained a generous goodbye gift of $500 cash. I still remember how thick and reassuring that white envelope was. It filled my hand. Almost certainly they intended this gift to help us pay for gas and other things that need to be shed and then bought again when you uproot and move across the country. Things which practical, future-thinking people would do with bonus money.

We drove straight to the James Art Studio in Saskatoon and bought "Chepwa Point" by Glen Veeman and "Open Country" by Terry Lindsay. Both pieces are art of place—they remind us what is wild and open and grows in blues and greens in the prairies. They remind us of our time there, which was dearly spent. The two of them have hung together for years now, and made all the spaces that were to come more pleasing; and for us, more beautiful and hospitable. They mark a time and place.

More art followed. We have marked milestones with small paintings; we have paid by installment, $50 a month for however many months; we have saved for some and splurged for others. Brent was once paid by way of a mountain watercolor, a delicate and light piece for all the rock it represents, because he helped a friend move scaffolding as Peter painted a huge mural in downtown Halifax.

We have not bought some things so that we could buy these things. Forgone this, for that. We've found pieces that delighted us at yard sales and scooped them up before someone else could spot their beauty behind that old toaster oven. We hung them.

Those are the easier pieces to explain. As a couple in ministry, it can sometimes feel that we've been caught untoward in the act of owning art. Thirty years married now, I still feel I need to explain.

"Who's the artist?" people sometimes ask, when they come into our space for the first time. "Oh, we've collected things here and there," we might say. "Brent's friend Paul painted those chickadees. Aren't they amazing?" I will over-talk about how buying art is accessible if you pay in installments, or barter or, even better, befriend. Or don't buy whiskey or sports equipment or good leather coats. "This one was a gift..."

...

Lauren Winner writes about this very thing in an essay called "The Art Patron: Someone who Can't Draw a Straight Line Tries to Defend her Art-Buying Habit" in *For the Beauty of the Church*, a collection of pieces edited by W. David O. Taylor, a pastor and author who has done so much to further the conversation about art(s) in the Church. She tells the story of being confronted by a reader disturbed by a passage in her memoir *When Girl Meets God*, where Winner writes about purchasing a piece of pricey art, and how could she justify that as a Christian.

Winner justifies it fully in the chapter that follows, while acknowledging the inherent privilege of anyone being able to buy art now and then. She writes, "...Scripture makes clear that God is interested in art. If you doubt that, turn to Exodus 26 and see how much space is devoted to the details of the tabernacle."

I did turn, and it really does. Old Testament linen is finely woven, the clasps are golden, the designs on curtains are exquisite and the thread is blue, purple and scarlet, on purpose. That's what God requested. Beauty matters. It's okay for space to be lovely and alive with art. "A Christian understanding of art involves a recognition that art does things," she writes. "In our Christian history, art mattered." And, of course, artists matter. Because I'm a Christian, I feel like Christian artists particularly and especially matter, as they do their work, pausing and painting and pointing.

I think we also feel we have to explain our art simply because we are a pastor and a writer. Pastors feel this way about a lot of things that might seem abundant. Is this house too nice? The car too new? It's just a creature-comfort-conflict-conundrum that is real for almost every pastor with a sensitive heart I have ever met.

And art, in particular, which is not necessary for anyone to own, is most understandable in grander houses owned by richer people. It's expected there, but surprising here. And yet the pen and the brush and the paint and clay and the mandolin and the Word made flesh all tie together so pleasingly. The Creator created all the creators who are creating—and that is all of us in some form, the cake-bakers and the garden-planters too—and then visited the creation in person, to make a lot of things abundantly clear. It is good to number art among the things we love.

•••

In two churches now, Brent has formed committees, talked together about artful things and then created gallery space. Church walls which stood in entrance lobbies, normally hung with evacuation directions and fire extinguishers or else nothing at all, are now gallery walls. They have become actual, legitimate gallery space inside church buildings where artists of faith can show their work.

It's such an elegant idea. I don't know what it's like for the artists, but I know it's wonderful for the rest of us. To pause and ponder at a painting. To read the little cards that guide and explain. Clustered together, each painting is like a chapter of a book, leading one to another and hinting at a larger, more complete story.

We have openings and gallery hours and the shows come and go. Artists can sell and people can buy. But most importantly, perhaps, people can look. We can see and be moved in that way that art does, by inviting us into a layered and beautiful story. Someone else's devotion can remind us and guide us forward or inward. A lot of us need that kind of "let me take you by the hand and look at where I am pointing" kind of help. Our church's art gallery is called The Lobby Gallery, because, yes, it's in the lobby, but also because art can be an entryway into faith. Step in, and behold.

Art, real, visible, and concrete in front of us, mysteriously reminds us there is more than just what we can touch and see.

The show at our church these days is full of big, expansive pieces done with vivid strokes and sweeping movements of Blaine Rancourt's arm. Or at least, that's how I imagine the making, because part of beholding art is also usually wondering however did they make this?

We know this artist, a little bit, and so when my book came out, Brent suggested we send a copy to him. He sent a note back to say there was a painting from that very show that reminded him of my work. He told us which one. The next Sunday, I went and found it, and now every Sunday, I visit it. I stand in front of it for a few moments, and I feel amazed again, at what art can do.

Karen Stiller
Writer & Editor

NOT LIKE GOING, BUT LIKE GOING BACK

Erika Veurink

> The sweetest thing in all my life has been the longing—to reach the Mountain, to find the place where all the beauty came from—my country, the place where I ought to have been born. Do you think it all meant nothing, all the longing? The longing for home? For indeed it now feels not like going, but like going back.
>
> —C.S. Lewis, *Till We Have Faces*

I MET C.S. LEWIS on the afternoon of my kindergarten graduation. His full-color, illustrated box set of the *Chronicles of Narnia* was a gift from my parents. It was a gift I anticipated receiving. I'd asked for it after spotting it at Barnes and Noble months earlier. It's hard to know what drew me to it, resting atop a tall shelf. Maybe it was the way my mom's eyes lifted in recognition, the utterly grown-up mossy green set behind a gold script? The glossy collectors' box held seven books tight in a row, impossible to fit back in once they were out.

I carried my unwrapped, sharp cornered mass of stories upstairs to my bedroom and shook the box until they spilled out. In the afternoon sun, buzzing from sheet cake, my blue paper cap still on my head, I wasted no time. I was careful to open the books from the edges to create no evidence of my visitation. I couldn't read the words or make sense of the otherworldly animals in the tiny paintings, but the strangeness startled my young mind.

That night, my mom started *The Magician's Nephew* at the foot of my bunk bed. I watched the book's spine crack, the pages bend, and felt the lightheadedness I now associate with infatuation. The damage had been done—the apple bitten into, the rock struck. I had become a citizen of C.S. Lewis's imagination, indelibly.

There was the Bible and then there was Narnia. I couldn't imagine needing anything else. By then, Bible stories had lost their luster. The giants felt small. The plagues had been tamed into Sunday School choruses. I could turn to John 3:16 in my worn out NIV with my eyes closed. But Narnia invited me into a wilder world. And it's true that the first stories are always the best stories. But Lewis's really were—moth balls, crunchy snow, always winter, never Christmas, dragons out of the velvet sea, water to gold, weeklong feasts, birds that were really lions or birds that were really witches. There was more saturation than I could hardly stomach. My suburban ecosystem of driveways and soybean fields and pledges to the Christian flag, was television fuzz in the light of its lucid color. To feel lost, swept up and swept in, was bliss.

A few years later, after many rounds of reading through the series, some on CDs blaring in the bumpy backseat of road trips, others under the quilted roof of a fort on a snow day, I protracted my inspiration outward. I adapted *The Lion, the Witch, and the Wardrobe* into an hour-long play. I spoke the lines as I scribbled desperately into a leftover composition notebook from fourth grade. I cast neighbors, siblings, cousins, even a stranger I met at the park—Mr. Tumnus was a minor role, anyway. I crafted costumes from the dress up bin. I hung paint splattered sheets from the rafters of the freezing basement storage room. An orphaned door, leftover from a renovation, felt predestined for the production.

But then I let it go, slid the script under my bed, and called the whole thing off. There was no performance or applauding audience. It was the creation I was concerned with. The cement floor of the storage room stage was my own expanding universe. I felt there would be hundreds more plays to write, a thousand more shocks of inspiration. When I called it good, I felt like Lewis, or God looking at the created expanse of his imagination. I was the first artist to raise a brush to a canvas. I was the hovering waters and the crackling earth and there was only forward. And forward was homeward.

I copied, "I believe in Christianity as I believe the sun has risen, not only because I see it, but because by it I see everything else," from *Mere Christianity* into a leather-bound notebook all the way in California the summer before college. I attended a two-week worldview summit, a sort of symposium on Christian belief. The sun that covered every inch of the college campus felt spiritual. We spent hours being lectured on old earth theories, the ramifications of free will, on slow truth and slippery slopes. At night, we gathered in small groups to rehash the day's topics. Knowledge felt addictive. Knowledge felt like something I could own and amass. It took the place of my chief joy from creation quietly, through easy-to-remember mnemonics and arguments won.

I read *Surprised by Joy* during breaks on the manicured lawn in front of the lecture hall. Like Lewis, I lost a parent at a young age. My steadfast, shimmering comfort shrunk to the size of a sympathy card. The soft corners of belief felt indulgent in contrast to the sharpness of grief. I turned to dusty theologians, their symmetrical and hard-won understandings of God. Imagination was childish. Why entertain anything when I could own certainty? Nuance felt pointlessly indulgent, not stark enough to fix anything. Narnia felt shelved back into the decorative box it arrived in.

The mastering of grief became my obsession. I looked first to the man who taught me worldbuilding in an attempt to reassemble my own. I started with one of the three copies of *A Grief Observed* I'd been given after my dad's funeral. I let the volume of passages like, "Feelings, and feelings, and feelings. Let me try thinking instead. From the rational point of view, what new factor has H.'s death introduced into the problem of the universe," drown out the beauty of quieter, less assertive moments in the book, like, "We cannot understand. The best is perhaps what we understand least."

When I moved to New York for college, my binder of lecture notes from just a few months prior, slid under my twin size dorm bed. I walked the steamy late-August streets in distrust at the sheer mass of the belief I felt. The willingness to try everything and the eagerness to love everyone felt at once unexpected and ancient. The world was mine to revel in. I got to decide what came with me from that binder, what truths and frameworks could begin to support the lush improbability of life after doctrine. Lewis wrote that an image of a faun carrying parcels in a snowy wood he had at sixteen was the inspiration for *The Lion, the Witch, and the Wardrobe,* which he began at forty. That's what it felt like in New York—familiar, divinely inspired, and at long last.

This new feeling needed a new language. I wanted new teachers, ones who looked like me and ones who didn't. I wanted a new vernacular, one that echoed the first expression which was never words but choruses of fantastic brightness. Lewis's limited perspective felt in opposition to the bendy and encompassing expansion the city shuffled me into. I didn't recognize him there. I wanted poets and neuroscientists and crossing guards to show me God. New York had no shortage of teachers.

The bus system and its haphazard gusts of smoke, the flight patterns of pigeons, watching the sunrise when I hadn't realized it had set. It all joined in a chorus louder, more moving than any lecture.

I didn't even think to mourn the belief system of my childhood. It never crossed my mind to decide what of those weekend retreats and summer camp rituals I would bring with me. In letters of Lewis's, reading beyond his canon and into his more intimate exchanges, I hoped to find a side of a man I long revered. What I found was quieter, less brandish in its certainty than some of his most acclaimed commentaries. Life was expanding rapidly and constantly and worth being awoken to every day ten times over. This new understanding had to come at the cost of the old. The death of gods was simply an adverse effect. For life was nothing without death.

> For poetry to spread its wings fully, there must be, besides the believed religion, a marvellous that knows itself as myth. For this to come about, the old marvellous, which once was taken as fact, must be stored up somewhere, not wholly dead, but in a winter sleep, waiting its time. If it is not so stored up, if it is allowed to perish, then the imagination is impoverished. Such a sleeping-place was provided for the gods by allegory. Allegory may seem, at first, to have killed them; but it killed only as the sower kills, for gods, like other creatures, must die to live.
>
> —C.S. Lewis, *The Allegory of Love*

Years later, it was in rereading *Narnia* to two boys I adore that I began to see Lewis like the first time. Not as a teacher or theologian, but as once a child himself. In youth, there was nothing to deem holy or otherwise. It all just *was*. There is a whimsy in "Jack's" work, just under the surface, dancing about, quietly carrying. It's easily missed in his later writing, stuffed under his English sensibility and pragmatic declarations. But in returning and imagining, as he deems all religion really is, he was there, playing. His reverence for myths, for the patterns they honored in the ever-expanding imagination of God, never wavered. He even wrote, "Someday you will be old enough to start reading fairy tales again."

I thought I wanted C.S. Lewis to be an oracle. I wanted his words to be infallible gospel. What I realized was that I didn't want that level of absolute from anyone, not really. The first sounds that set the world into motion had to have been questions. There was light and it danced. There was water and it expanded. There was dust and it calcified into a person, into nations, into thousands of traceable threads. At the very center of truth, there are no gatekeepers. There are wanderers and pilgrims and seekers. And they have their stories. There is life and death. There are dragons and false gods and cloudy stretches. But the dragons are really misunderstood boys, tempted by shimmering things. The false gods look sturdier the further away they stand; the weaker the closer you are. And the cloudy stretches, the charcoal smudge seasons of half dreams, are just the "unfocused gleam of divine truth falling on human imagination."

Erika Veurink
Writer & MFA Student

OF ART AND AGE

Ronna Bauman

"HOPE IS THE THING WITH FEATHERS," I write confidently, the strokes of my pen brandished like a strutting peacock. An old friend sent me this treasure a few years ago, a well-known nugget from Emily Dickinson's trove, and I often pay it forward: "Hope is the thing with feathers / That perches in the soul / And sings the tune without the words / And never stops at all." I inject the lines into a note for a friend—an offering in the midst of her waiting, and points for me: clearly, I'm cultured, for I quote poetry.

Dickinson's lines, much like Tennyson and Longfellow and even Dr. Seuss, are nourishment to my soul, yet this particular poem's symbolism is far from lofty, despite my self-congratulation. The metaphor is conspicuous and the author's intent is clear, even from the outset. A sucker for iambic pentameter, I grabbed onto this little jewel precisely because it is simple, catchy, approachable. Because it *rhymes!*

I appreciate when art is accessible, handed to me like warm tea in a familiar mug, its purpose void of mystery. But I have five children aged 19 to 27, and lately, I find their art is not so easily grasped. I often feign my comprehension of the books, poems, and films that they're eager to share. The art that woos my kids can feel more to me like a spiced whiskey with a bitterness that I am unprepared for. When I encounter the daunting flavors that compel my children, I put down the glass, lay aside the anthology, tune out the music, or pivot in the gallery with a silent sigh, disappointed in myself that the beauty feels out of reach.

•••

I thought I was deep, but am I actually *(gasp)* shallow? Their tastes make me wonder, "Why does this feel like a too-heavy lift for me?" Me, who often disappeared into corners of my house to scribble prose as a young girl, nursing a belief that I possessed a monopoly on the good, the beautiful, and the true. My poetry, bursting with eloquence, would one day be famous, thought my nine-year-old self. But 45 years later, poetry sometimes eludes me, and I wonder if this is a hint of something I haven't quite grasped about myself?

Perhaps I'm not alone. Certain work feels inaccessible to many viewers and readers, I'm sure. Doesn't *The New Yorker* elude many of us? This bastion of literary high-mindedness lands in our mailbox weekly, nestled between coupon flyers and utility bills. The iconic graphics and social commentary arrive because our son—an aspiring journalist—subscribed in order to receive the free tote bag and occasional literary inspiration. As I flip through the pages of the 47 issues per year that take turns on my kitchen counter, I wonder to myself about the kind of reader who slogs her way to the articles' end. Like so much art, the on-ramp feels too steep. Instead, I settle for strategically placing a few of these souvenirs in the bathroom basket, to impress my guests.

•••

To be fair, arts and letters should indeed offer the world an invitation to ponder. In one of my favorite cinematic moments,

Robin Williams's character in *Dead Poets Society* mesmerizes his students with the allure of Walt Whitman:

> We don't read and write poetry because it's cute. We read and write poetry because we are members of the human race. And the human race is filled with passion. And medicine, law, business, engineering, these are noble pursuits and necessary to sustain life. But poetry, beauty, romance, love, these are what we stay alive for.
>
> To quote from Whitman, "O me! O life! of the questions of these recurring; of the endless trains of the faithless, of cities fill'd with the foolish...what good amid these, O me, O life?" Answer. That you are here—that life exists, and identity; that the powerful play goes on and you may contribute a verse. That the powerful play goes on and you may contribute a verse. What will your verse be?

Professor Keating's speech cuts us to the quick, rallying us to stand on our desks in defiance of all that lacks depth. He evokes a war cry: "Give us the *arts!*" Yet, if I'm honest, in the face of refined literature, with its big words, sometimes I feel so...*small.*

When my children "get it," I applaud them. But it's simultaneously salt in the wound for me, the mom who dragged all five of them to museums and concerts in every city we relocated. As a transitory military wife, I've gaped wide-eyed in galleries and cathedrals all over the world—I have cultural street cred, for heaven's sake! So I admit, it feels unfair that so often, one generation down might see what I can't see, and hear what I can't hear among today's creatives.

•••

"Why do you get it, and I don't?" I wonder out loud. "Does it feel," my 22-year-old daughter kindly suggests, "like you *haven't done the work?*" She generously offers that sometimes, she can relate.

She's nailed it. It feels like I haven't done the work. Like it's my fault. It evokes the unwelcome return of that monster I try to slay—it evokes *shame*.

The poem that's laborious for me to interpret? "Well," I scold myself, "it's because I didn't spend my twenties reading The Great Books." I'm ashamed that I talk a big game about culture with the artistic young people in my life, but haven't actually read Wilde's *The Picture of Dorian Gray*. Never mind that my early twenties had me navigating another country and a new community as an overseas Air Force wife, learning the art of marriage. Never mind that I was working and raising the very children who now outsmart me. The inner critic wins the day.

For what is shame's twin, if not *regret?* And the language of regret is "the shoulds." I should have sought that master's degree. I should have connected to the downtown art scene. I should have frequented film festivals and read *Anna Karenina*. I should have taken up photography, posted my songs on Sound-cloud, joined a writers' circle. I march in line with so many of my generation to the cadence of shame and regret, the rhythm beating in my mind that I must be *dumb*. I feel dumb in the light of this great work.

Perhaps my fellow fifty-somethings would agree heartily, or perhaps I'm the only one that resonates with Walt Whitman's description, "of myself forever reproaching myself." Despite my academic training, it's a formidable task to follow the latest strains of existential thought when dinner won't make itself. Often, the sliver of time I've saved to curl up with a blanket and reading glasses turns into the task of rereading lofty allusions as my mind wanders like a toddler to tomorrow's to-do list.

Nonetheless, Wendell Berry offers a gentle answer to my self-chafing. He writes: "The mind that is not baffled is not employed. The impeded stream is the one that sings." *Art is supposed to baffle us.* And if my mind is the impeded stream, I will invite the obstructions. The low-hanging fruit is not always the most delicious.

Are not magic and mystery intertwined? We should strain to sharpen our senses, to ponder the creators' intent, to grow in empathy, and to cultivate an eye for hidden meaning. To ask one another, "How did this film / image / verse land with you?" As my oldest son affirms, "I respect art that I don't understand— even if I don't understand it, I'm glad it's there; it widens the landscape."

•••

Outside of Oxford's famed Blackwell's bookstore, I once saw a chalkboard with a phrase that I often ponder: "The purpose of art is washing the dust of daily life off our souls. —Pablo Picasso." The dust of "daily life" gets thicker the more "dailys" one has under her belt. This is all the more reason for those who boast more days and decades to give ourselves grace—to approach seemingly unapproachable art with eagerness, seeking a good washing. As Christ followers, it's with clean souls that we are free to celebrate mystery, to be confused, to "not get it," and to enjoy the goodness of the Lord in the land of the living, in whatever form that takes. We need one another—old and young—to wash off the dust together.

Community offers the crucial kaleidoscope in which to cherish beauty with a more discerning eye, ear, heart, mind. This morning, my daughter texted me a Rainer Maria Rilke poem. It isn't simple. There's no iambic pentameter. It doesn't even rhyme. But Rilke has significantly stirred her and her siblings, even and often to tears, so this window to her heart was a gift. She graced me with it in hopes that I'll press on in a space to which she knows God is inviting me. She graced me with it to help wash off the dust, so I may more clearly see, feel, hear:

> Each mind fabricates itself.
>
> We sense its limits, for we have made them.
>
> And just when we would flee them, you come
>   and make of yourself an offering.
>
> I don't want to think a place for you.
>
> Speak to me from everywhere.
>
> Your Gospel can be comprehended
>   without looking for its source

"Speak to me from everywhere." From pages and canvases and television screens, God speaks to and beckons us. Though beauty is baffling, he dispels shame and "shoulds" because he comes to us. As impeded streams, we have limits, but we need not flee. Eventually these impediments will lead to a new tune, singing of our Creator's beauty.

So I'll keep leaning in, in my fifties, in my eighties. Because this gives me hope. And "hope is the thing with feathers, that perches in the soul."

Ronna Bauman
Mother & Communications Manager

HANDKERCHIEFS EVERYWHERE

Abbey Sitterley

WE HAD EACH SIGNED UP for early classes that spring semester. On Tuesday and Thursday mornings at 6:30, Emily would pick me up in her rusty red sedan with the heat half broken and we'd make our way to the FLCC campus. Emily's schedule consisted of a series of preliminary lectures for a nursing capstone, and mine, a mix of liberal arts courses including Reiki. But as we neared midterms, I developed a secret. Like always, I'd stand outside in the pre-dawn cold with two coffees, take the shivering thirty-minute ride to campus, wave goodbye to Emily at the nursing wing and then proceed to skip all my morning classes. It wasn't that I was lazy, it was more like theft: I was stealing away.

Not long before, one of my closest friends in the New Age movement had given me Madeleine L'Engle's book, *Walking on Water: Reflections on Faith and Art* and I'd been devouring it. As the thoroughly rebellious child of two former Sunday School teachers, I embraced anything that called the religion of my childhood small-minded, opting to delve deep into a relativistic interpretation of spirituality instead. But L'Engle was different than the typical Christian author. Instead of proselytizing, she merely explained that the doctrines of Christianity gave intrinsic spiritual worth to creativity. Not only were we image-bearers of God, we were called to partake as co-creators in the world. And as co-creators, we had to humbly admit that our work isn't really ours, but rather a profound gift of God's goodness and divine will.

For a young writer searching for meaning, this was a seismic shift. Christianity, despite its abrasive truth claims and stale traditions, was deeper, more enticing, and intellectually satisfying than just an ancient moral code. My morning Reiki elective be damned, I'd much rather feed this new appetite than monitor my classmate's auras. And so I strolled down to the library basement and tucked myself away into a small connecting passageway with L'Engle. Flanked by floor-to-ceiling windows on each side, the morning sun would warm this little space like a greenhouse and I'd lay on a wood bench reading for hours, marveling at how Jesus might actually know what He's doing.

I stole away to this nook whenever I could, my backpack smuggling in new books that only drew me deeper.

Eventually, Flannery O'Connor's short stories found themselves in tow. Stories like "The Turkey," "The Life You Save May Be Your Own," and "Revelation" shocked and unnerved me. Here was God as the Hound of Heaven staring down characters caught between the paws of grace, trying to wiggle free to no avail. I saw much of myself in Ruller's false piety, Ruby Turpin's pride, as well as Shiflet's self-serving proclivities, and felt just as, in O'Connor's terms, 'Christ-haunted' as the south they were set in. As deeply gothic fiction, O'Connor's stories are clearly crafted to neither comfort nor convert. Rather, they merely escort the reader to meet the startling contrast of man before his Maker and promptly abandon one there. Such raw looks at the sublime were gilded all the same, shining in my eyes much like L'Engle's words did. But this time I felt out of breath, as if being chased.

These encounters weren't limited to text. I began watching The *X-Files* for its reputation as a cult classic sci-fi series and found that same spiritual longing underpinning the show's entire framework. For those of us who get dizzy in the chasm between faith and doubt, the tagline phrase "I want to believe" is a touchstone, something that can be leaned into when we don't have the strength to will much more. Mulder's unslakable thirst for truth alongside Scully's empirically driven skepticism mirrored the same tension happening in my own heart. I couldn't escape it. Chris Carter, creator of *The X-Files,* is not a religious man, nor is the show religious in nature, and yet it kindled the same desire L'Engle and O'Connor's words stirred in me. How can such disparate themes and mediums deliver the same divine impression? Is it we who pull meaning out of these things or is creativity itself imbued with echoes of the first Creator?

Frederick Buechner once wrote, "In His holy flirtation with the world, God occasionally drops a handkerchief. These handkerchiefs are called saints." When I look back on my life, I see such works as *Walking on Water, The Collected Short Stories, The X-Files,* and many others like carefully dropped handkerchiefs. While these creators were certainly not saints, nor their works necessarily saintly, they were used by God in His "holy flirtation" with me. Their place in my story is intentional if not completely integral. How else could I feel the same pull across mediums and voices, fiction and nonfiction, religious and secular? I had no desire for the things of the God I left, and yet, behind every voice I turned to, He called me. Every beautiful thing spoke of Him. Every place I visited, He haunted. And so my conversion was not via evangelistic conversation or a factual argument, but the Creator's unbridled wooing across the spectrum of creativity.

Singer-songwriter Andrew Peterson, in his latest book *Adorning the Dark: Thoughts on Community, Calling, and the Mystery of*

Making, explores how art can be the catalyst for a real movement in the human spirit. Peterson explains, "Something as real as a tectonic shift might be happening in their magnificent soul, like the mechanism of a primal clock ticking closer and closer to the triumphant sounding of the bell tower, a revelation, a scattering of birds...something that reminds them of the grand mystery of their selfhood."

Ecclesiastes 3:11 says that God "has put eternity into man's heart...." Art has an unparalleled ability to touch this eternity hidden within us. We feel this intrinsically when we experience great stories, or have our minds enraptured by some visual masterpiece: that heady mix of jealousy and inspiration, the rush to get home right away and start again, a step out of time and into a flow state that drags on until it's done with us. Our existential longing is vast and amorphous, but it is art that gives us language for it, enabling us to process and understand the big questions of eternity. These moments break up our fallow ground and spur us onward, causing us to remember that we are indeed, a soul.

Consider the experience of renowned director Krzysztof Kieslowski. In his memoir *Kieslowski on Kieslowski,* he recalls, "At a meeting just outside Paris, a fifteen-year-old girl came up to me and said that she'd been to see my movie. She'd gone once, twice, three times and only wanted to say one thing really...that she realized that there is such a thing as a soul. She hadn't known before, but now she knew that the soul does exist. There's something very beautiful in that. It was worth making *Véronique* for that girl. It was worth working for a year, sacrificing all that money, energy, time, patience, torturing yourself, killing yourself, making thousands of decisions, so that one young girl in Paris should realize that there is such a thing as a soul. It's worth it."

Kieslowski saw the influence film has on the interior life of the viewer. What eludes us in the realm of fact and explanation flies to us sweetly through image, sound, and story. Can we ever place our finger on when God begins to move on the heart? The girl in Kieslowski's memory has realized she has a soul. Perhaps months, even years after such a revelation, she may learn that her soul is a created thing. Perhaps someday she'll find herself drawn into greater knowledge of that soul's landscape, the God who made it, and the life to be lived in response. Secular art made by unredeemed hands is not safe from the God who draws His people to Himself. When the decisive inbreak occurs, the fruit is always heavy on the vine.

Though He takes joy in it, God does not need an author's permission to use their endeavors for His purpose. Creativity, like all creation, is His subject and He will do with it as He wills. The Lord is the Lord of all: our existential longings, our salvation, and our craft. We can see there is an everlasting dance happening in the core of creativity, carrying its viewer further up and further in toward divine revelation, and Christian creatives are invited to learn the steps. All things trumpet the coming Lord who works in mysterious ways. So should our work.

Yet this is not a conscription. God's wooing of the world will go on with or without us. He will use bad art and good art, *New York Times* bestsellers and campus zines, abstract expressionism and pop music, arthouse films and Instagram poetry, even good questions in atheistic manifestos and a small town Sunday sermon. Handkerchiefs are everywhere. Who knows? Someone might find one while hiding in a library basement while earning a bad grade in Reiki.

Abbey Sitterley
Writer & Musician

CREATION

A HEAVY, BEAUTIFUL BURDEN

Eniola Abioye

Our crown has already been bought and paid for.
All we have to do is wear it.

James Baldwin

I DON'T REMEMBER THE FIRST TIME I saw Basquiat's name or a piece of artwork with the iconic crown. I recall being put off by how fierce his scrawls were. I remember wondering why someone would call that art. I was overwhelmed by the scribblings, I didn't understand. They reminded me too much of the world around me.

I heard stories of young girls being kidnapped in Nigeria, economies supported by pillars of human trafficking in Southeast Asia, and European nations drowning in alcohol abuse. Stateside, families being torn apart by political opinions, like something reminiscent of the Civil War, while urban cities experience food deserts, shortages, and water crises, and wealthier communities are overrun by suicide and opium overdoses.

And still, there are stories of soldiers coming home, families being reunited, children getting into their dream school, and marginalized people groups defeating the odds.

The complexities are jarring.

•••

I like to wander through my local art museum. I try to take my time with a specific category of expression. I study not only the works themselves, but my own reaction to the work. I felt quieted, reflective, and sobered by art. Everything from the use of colors during the specific time period to the subject matter. Everything from the shading practices, whether the artist is male or female. Learning the stories of the artists and the events that took place during their work's release. All of this helped provide context and understanding for their art. It is easy to look at a collection of paintings and sculptures and make assumptions about their significance, but it takes humility to understand.

There can be much pretension surrounding art. For me, art has become an opportunity to invite people into narratives and conversations that typically require emotional charge or complex concepts.

In 2019, I worked for a nonprofit organization that serves a network of underserved communities in the Dallas-Fort Worth, Texas, area. We took a group of about 15 high school students to New Orleans and visited an art gallery called StudioBe. An artist named Brandan "BMIKE" Odums had filled a 30,000 square foot warehouse with enormous canvas and wall masterpieces of black activists, motifs, and victims of police brutality and racially motivated crimes.

As I wandered through, I was moved by the reverence and honor of the victims. Haloed portraits of Oscar Grant and Trayvon Martin holding the "I AM A MAN" signs noted during the Million Man March during the 1960s, colorful backdrops with pictures of Muhammad Ali, and other celebrity activists. There were FBI transcripts of Dr. Martin Luther King Jr's conversations plastered on one of the walls beside an old-school phone. The artist also used pieces of the walls from homes destroyed during Hurricane Katrina as canvas to pay homage to his homeland.

But out of all of it, what caught my attention were the spray-painted three-point crowns between quotation marks that accompanied Odums's signature and sometimes represented in for his signature. The symbol reminded me of Jean-Michael Basquiat's signature three-point crown.

About half a year ago, I was studying up on Jean-Michel Basquiat's life and art. Tension, question, and commentary filled his canvases and sketchbooks. I realized that sometimes, we don't give ourselves permission to process tension. Hence, my initial reaction to his work.

One of his most predominant symbols was a crown. A three point crown, roughly drawn, typically filled with the color yellow, hovering over a figure. Sometimes the crown was suspended above nothing, but it constantly carried the weight of the beauty and pain of being black in America.

•••

I am Nigerian. Nigeria is in West Africa. I was born in the United Kingdom. Camden to be specific, but I grew up in the United States. Beginning in New York, then Florida, then the largest chunk of my childhood in Atlanta, with a year and a half in Tulsa, Oklahoma, and after, returning back to Atlanta. I graduated high school in Charlotte, North Carolina. After two years of college in Oklahoma, I moved alone to Dallas, Texas, believing I was following this invisible yellow brick road to my purpose. I landed in Dallas, and ultimately found myself at a Bible school. Over the next decade of my life, I would hear the distant call for justice for members of the African Diaspora (people of African descent). I would sense how the call was larger than hashtags and slogans, but a deep longing in God's heart to see the lost reconciled, first back to Him, then to one another.

As an African, the weight of that complexity overwhelmed me, and I wasn't sure how to progress. This was one of those things you can't sit back and watch play out. One, because it is part of my story, and rejecting it would communicate a form of self-hatred. Two, because it is important to God to join the narrative of reconciliation. The Scriptures speak of ministers of reconciliation. It is part of our inheritance as new creations to lean into this ministry. The hulking HOW was then the most daunting undertaking before me. How do I step into a narrative with so much history, pain, and opinion? What space do I take in this story? After joining the chorus of vocal pundits on social media, I got quiet and learned that God wanted me to take up the space I was made to take up.

•••

One day, I was sitting with my parents and began to ask them about their families and how they grew up. After a series of humorous stories, eye-opening conversations, and tender moments, my mom and dad told me how they both had royal blood in their respective villages in southwest Nigeria. They came from a line of king-makers: a group of people who sit on a council and decide the next chief or monarch of their community.

Interestingly enough, years before that, during my senior year of high school, my father changed our family's last name to "Abioye," a Nigerian name that means royalty from "Ogun-tona," a Nigerian name meaning "god of iron." He did this at the request of his late father, Samuel Abioye Oguntona. It seemed like God was weaving my story into His the whole time.

•••

I almost lost my mind when I realized Marvel was releasing a black superhero film. It was over a year before the release date when I saw the first teaser, and I remember crying and trying to replay it as many times as possible. I think it was during a Super Bowl Commercial. It was a full year before I would watch it. As someone who prides themselves in not jumping at the latest trends, I danced to the theaters opening night and watched the movie not once, not twice, but seven times, and each time I watched symbolism play out. I watched as a newly crowned African king took ownership of the lost people of his continent and began the road to reconciliation through the royalty he won. Having a crown meant serving his people on a massive scale. Our questions, our tension appear like unexpected house guests, and we find ourselves fumbling for the best way to host.

However, I find that Jesus's response to tension, questions, and even political commentary was to create. Instead of trying to solve the solution like a tenured mathematician, he chose to create. When asked about the Kingdom, Jesus responded with a story. Not song. Not a poem. Not a piece of new technology. But a story composed to carry within it, the deepest and simplest meanings. Isn't it fascinating how if you told a child the story of Goldilocks and the Three Bears, they would hear the message without you ever needing to preach it to them?

Sometimes I wonder if Jesus had his parables memorized or if they were free-styled. When asked, "Who is my neighbor?" He offered a tale riddled with racial tension. And when asked why He would allow a known immoral woman to wash his feet with her tears, He responded with a story about two debtors. Possibly implying that this woman was not the only known sinner, but also the one asking him the question. Jesus chose story as a weapon. He crowned his truths with creativity, with a story. When God hovered over chaotic darkness before time began, He made a decision. He chose to speak light. He chose to create.

Cultural complexities, political pundits, and frustrating opinions are nothing new and are going nowhere, but sons and daughters of God are equipped to tell a different story. Responses of presence, courage, and hope that look like intention-filled words and color in poetry, film, art, and song. During the Civil Rights Era, many marched, many sang. Songs penned by the men and women who stood beside their peers declaring a new future, with their words. Others sculpted, while others painted. Artists are prophets. They carry a banner that reminds all with breath in their lungs of a probable future headed their way.

Maybe this is the invitation of today. To dig through the tragedy and glory of our stories, to take inventory of our passion and purpose, and create. Create the future we desire to live. To remind ourselves of the life of a co-laborer with God, one who longs to comprehend what He sees and create a future He is in. Like Abraham, who sojourned looking for a place whose builder and maker was God. If you are overwhelmed by complexity and tension, create. Your creativity is a crown given to you by God, so pick it up and wear it.

Eniola Abioye
Writer & Musician

THE ANALOGY OF
THE ARCHER

Erika Veurink

I FOUND MYSELF ON THE EDGE of a wooded expanse of Northern Minnesota, lined up with a group of other eleven-year-old girls. Our parents had signed us up for the archery excursion at Christian summer camp. Targets were taped to hay bales in the distance. The first arrows I launched fell a few feet in front of me. A counselor leaned over my shoulder, "Your power has to come from pulling back." Her advice didn't lead to my mastery that day, but it has stuck with me ever since.

Creative life functions largely the same way. It helps me to identify three separate movements: retreat, aim, and imagine. Every artist has a phase they prefer over the others. I have some writer friends who can't bear the weight of publication. The finality feels crushing. Others, like myself, would happily spend the rest of their lives in ideation. Think of the way retreating, aiming, and imagining form one, seamless arc of creation into manifestation. When the days are long or the project has lost its romantic gleam, it helps to identify one's place in the analogy of the archer. Follow the prompts below based on where you're at presently, or where you hope to land.

RETREAT

No one can help you if you're stuck in a work. Only you can figure a way out, because only you see the work's possibilities. In every work, there's an inherent impossibility which you discover sooner or later some intrinsic reason why this will never be able to proceed. You can figure out ways around it. Often the way around it is to throw out, painfully, the one idea you started with.

—**Annie Dillard,**
Notes for Young Writers

Early morning, somewhere just outside of the dream state, there is there is a smooth surface of a new day—welcome to retreat. This is the time to pull your arrow back into your trusted rituals. Honor your obsessions, even if only to release them at the altar of a better idea. Remind yourself that this is creation. There's nothing precious about it. Even the Creation story started with dirt.

Retrace your steps: In a literal sense, what brought you to the work this morning? Make a map of your movement—describe the coffee, the quiet walk from your warm bed, the sounds. More abstractly, what are the projects/dreams/concepts that have led you to the front door of this work?

Consider the child self. What can you do without checking the clock? Spend time in this imaginative space. Take a walk with only your earliest concept to keep you company. Draw your dreams from the night before. Remember, Martin Buber said, "play is the exaltation of the possible." Go gently.

AIM

Aim at heaven and you will get earth thrown in.
Aim at earth and you get neither.

—**C.S. Lewis,**
Mere Christianity

Setting a course might be the least glamorous, most essential part of any artistic endeavor. It's easy to get swept up in the start, but without proper aim, the center can feel impossible. This middle act can be where it's hard to find inspiration. It can be hard to see how the toiling amounts to something sacred. Keep going. Every artist in every medium feels at least an ounce of this. Keeping an intentional aim will prevent you from relying on your emotions when the work feels insurmountable. Focus on your higher calling. Picture everything from a bird's eye view, and then slowly descend. You're making art, not running a race. Trust the hours.

Set a timer for 20 minutes. No distractions. Write without editing on a sheet of blank paper or an email draft to relieve the pressure of your work in context. Make a list of friends who support you. Make a list of friends whom you love, but can't support you. Make a final list of artists you aspire to create alongside.

IMAGINE

The function of art is to do more than tell it like it is—it's to imagine what is possible.

—**bell hooks,** *Outlaw Culture:*
Resisting Representations

Go further than you think you can. Push the edges of the piece until they push back. Then the work is ready for refinement.

Cut, toss, tear, burn. You're not finished until you know you are. It's not about you, the artist. It's about the work you're bringing forth. Once it's over, take time for reflection. Touch the indentation of where the arrow hit the target. Feel gratitude. Prepare yourself to begin again.

Write in the present tense about the highest life you could imagine for the work. Use specific details. Describe how it feels to have created something that lives beyond you. What would you create if you felt no responsibility?

Humble yourself. Read a book in a genre and author you aren't familiar with. Support living artists. Remain creatively ambidextrous. It'll keep you grounded. How can you become a beginner?

Erika Veurink

Writer & MFA

BEING OBEDIENT TO TIME

Rachel Marie Kang

MYONGHI KANG, A SOUTH KOREAN ARTIST, spent three decades working on a single painting. There, in the photo featured on a CNN segment where she shares her story, Kang stands poised as ever: her hands are unclenched and a look of contentment rests upon her face. Wispy strands of silver hair pose in delicate layers, and she is surrounded by two wall-sized canvases, all speckled in earth-tone shades of green, mauve, and brown.

"I would not dare say that I paint time," she recalls in a phone interview. "That would be very arrogant—but time is in what I paint. I let myself be the hands of time. I obey time, but do not try to manipulate it," she says.

Her words strike me with their poignance, but also offer a salve to my self-inflicted wound where I feel the constant ache of time slipping away. I am soothed by what she says; she has spoken into one of my deepest desires—to obey time rather than be overwhelmed by it.

A canvas hangs on the wall outside my kitchen. It is white and covered with thick strokes of a midnight blue that fade and altogether disappear. From one corner to another, the strokes reach upward in a sort of sea-like dance. And when

I wash dishes, from where I stand in the kitchen, I can see this incomplete, half-done painting. A familiar pang prompts within me, "I haven't finished my painting. I need to finish my painting."

Myonghi Kang tells the story of her painting, "Le temps des camélias" ("The Time of Camellias"), and how she started it while living in Paris's 19th arrondissement. A brushstroke here, a bit of blending there, she'd return to this painting again and again over the course of ten years. She would approach her canvas, not merely with color but with questions.

"I would go back to the painting with all these questions in my mind, and memories from traveling," she recalls. She held to this practice of pondering while painting until she eventually abandoned her project, saying that it never did come to feel finished. Ten years later, in South Korea's Jeju Island, Kang returned to her painting with renewed inspiration. Surrounded by camellias, she incorporated her surroundings into the art, adding layers of new life to her painting. Having started "Le temps des camélias" twenty years ago, Kang spent another ten years working on and eventually completing it in 2018.

•••

I think of my many personal projects, how I handle and manipulate them like spinning plates. I am breathless, running from one pole to another in an attempt to keep them all suspended and spinning. It is like a spectacle, a circus act. If I let one plate fall, I am a failure—in my work, in my art, in the ideas that tug at my heart.

As I write this, summer is turning its deep bend into August, that hazy month which is hot and humid but also hints at the repose of fall to come. Soon, leaves will leave trees and the days will grow shorter, darker, and colder. The earth will tilt on its axis and we will turn away from the heat of that glorious sun. And if we pay attention, really pay attention, we will notice in our own spirits a similar kind of seasonality. Along with the natural world, we, too, will turn inward. Our bodies will obey the shift in seasons, nature's clock that ticks and tells time. We will fall subject to schedules that we cannot outwit or control. We will withdraw through the long winter, that sleepy season where the world grows sleepy and silent and still.

"I obey time," says Kang. Her words resound in my chest. I want this for my life. I want this for my art, too. Is it not a universal craving, not a universal calling? That eternal ache within us nudging us toward noticing that we are in relation and in rhythm with something greater than ourselves. This is why we are in awe of the sun that rises and sets without fail. This is why winter, with its white-falling snow, enchants us. This is why the blooming camellias and roses speak to our souls in ways we will never understand.

We are captivated by a consistent, eternal clock, utterly dazzled by the simple truth that God is the one spinning our world in motion. He is the one who wills the winter and the one who sustains summer. He is the one who once spoke light into life and the one who determined the indispensability of darkness. Yes, even darkness.

Genesis 8:22 says, "As long as the earth endures, seedtime and harvest, cold and heat, summer and winter, day and night will never cease." The seasonality of this world, as long as the earth endures, is his promise to us. It is his way of instilling stability and his way of endorsing eternal rhythms of rest. It is his way of calling us close to his heart and showing us the way that he moves—the slow, deep way that he works.

•••

A few days ago, my friend, K.J. Ramsey, and I talked face-to-face through our phones. We sat there, telling each other about the seasons we find ourselves in—the lulls of life, the hiccups in health, and the time-consuming cultivation of our creativity. My eyes hold wells of water. K.J.'s presence is composed and calm. She tells me about a prayer by Pierre Teilhard de Chardin that's been strengthening her soul as of late.

"Above all," she reads, "trust in the slow work of God." The water in my eyes forms in the shallow of my lashes. She continues.

> "We are quite naturally impatient in everything to reach the end without delay. We should like to skip the intermediate stages. We are impatient of being on the way to something unknown, something new.
>
> "And yet it is the law of all progress that it is made by passing through some stages of instability—and that it may take a very long time.
>
> "And so I think it is with you; your ideas mature gradually—let them grow, let them shape themselves, without undue haste. Don't try to force them on, as though you could be today what time (that is to say, grace and circumstances acting on your own good will) will make of you tomorrow.
>
> "Only God could say what this new spirit gradually forming within you will be. Give Our Lord the benefit of believing that his hand is leading you, and accept the anxiety of feeling yourself in suspense and incomplete."

I cry in front of K.J., with visions flashing across the hidden places of my mind. I think of the house I want to build that is only a dream. I think of the songs I've written that are still not yet done. I think of the fictional character I am creating and how I carve out early mornings to seep out her story—but how there is never enough time because, in my mind, this story has to be alive and in the hands of readers right now.

I think and live as if I could eclipse time and make anything today what it can only be tomorrow. I consider the fear that engulfs me at the thought of willingly walking away from an unfinished work, and yet the beautiful faith that would require. I think of how out-of-control it might feel to be free from the pressure of figuring a thing out—a plot, a painting, a business venture in photography—and yet, unencumbered. I think of the risk, but also the rapture, of willingly suspending your art over a sea of unknown endings.

But what if seasonal winters in our art provide a pathway for the cultivation of creativity? What if art delayed by decades does not raise questions of competence? What if the only consequential concern is of our own becoming?

Perhaps the pause in your painting, the waiting in your writing, or the detour in your dancing, is an invitation to cultivate questions and curiosities, all of which are for you, all of which will deeply form not merely your art but your very being.

There is no rule that you must rush, there is no race of accomplishment to run. There is only coming to trust in the God who holds the temporality of our lives in his hands. There is coming to surrender to the seasonal nature of our world, our lives, our art. There is only finding ourselves in suspension, a waiting that looks less like waning and more like wondering. A pause that looks less like postponing and more like pondering the nature of our world and work—the nature of the work being done within us.

I see my painting on the wall outside my kitchen. It is incomplete and lacking, but it tells me something more than that. It communicates that I, too, am unfinished and wanting.

A swirling stroke of color on a canvas, fragmentary and on the way to being something not quite realized.

At least, not yet.

Rachel Marie Kang
Author & Artist

DON'T DO YOUR BEST

Karen Stiller

WHEN I WAS A GIRL, I sat for one long morning at an outdoor market behind a table full of earrings made from bright, plastic buttons. I don't know how I came up with this idea, or why I thought it was a good one, but I glued earring backs to dozens of sets of buttons and one Saturday my father drove me to the Sackville flea market. I don't remember if I sold even a single set, but I do remember I retired from jewelry making that very day, just past noon.

Humbled? Certainly. Deterred? Not at all. I bumbled my way from one craft to another for years, searching for instant excellence, fame, and fortune.

I dabbled in salt-clay Christmas ornaments, with seashells I crushed with my mother's rolling pin, as an innovation. I enrolled in a stained glass-making course with my handsome father who was the only man in class, with whom I watched mothers goofily flirt. I wasn't a cut-things-in-a-straight-line kind-of artist, that was clear. I moved on and moved to Vancouver. There, I abandoned soap-making, quickly, when I learned what lye feels like bubbling away on the soft flesh of the inner arm. Papermaking was wet and wonderful, but my lumpy sheets looked nothing like the fine linen stationary sold in the

Granville Market store that hosted the class. After not trying very hard with that either, I moved along.

Sometime around then I stumbled on a magazine for "Canadian crafters" in a hobby store I wandered through, searching for my next big thing. I had been writing for a few years by then, short pieces for small papers in tiny places, which I think is how writers should start—growing good, slowly. I wove the threads of my misadventures together into a piece called "Confessions of a Failed Crafter," and I made it onto the cover.

"Goodbye Crafting!" I said, and maybe forever, but I didn't know that yet for sure. "Bon voyage!" Crafting yelled back and slammed the door behind me. In writing, I discovered my clay, my paints, and my mandolin. Writing would be my art and my craft.

•••

"Sarah will boil our heads like cabbages," said Bonne, my editor, when I sent in another round of tweaks as my manuscript wrapped itself up.

Each time another set of almost-final proofs landed in my inbox, dread filled me. How long could I put off opening these email attachments? How weak would these pages be, lying before me on their stretcher?

Finally, I would convince myself to do the work one more time, every single word of the work, over and over, and only then I could go out for candy or coffee.

Not once did I add more weight to those pages. I substituted or subtracted only. Near the end, revision is almost always removal. I spotted the weeds. I dug down to the bottom of their roots, yanked, and smoothed the churned soil flat once again with the palm of my hand. I pulled and patted over and over and over, not until it was the best it could be, but until Bonne wrote back and said, "It's too late. Sorry. The files are at the printer."

I cleaned the dirt out from under my fingernails and washed my hands of it then, drying them off on a soft towel. A few weeks later I flew to Chicago—one of the last batches of Canadians to do that for a while—to record the audio version of my book.

I finally met up with the physical copy of my book when a publicist handed me an early review copy, and I discovered that I liked her. "You look great," I whispered into her ear.

I sat behind a wall in a make-shift sound booth, reading. One engineer turned dials and lowered levers, and the other read silently along with me. He was the police, ensuring I didn't alter a jot or a tittle. I delivered a bottle of maple syrup to Sarah, to say sorry and thank you, because maple syrup does both.

As I read out loud to two complete strangers over three complete days, there were still words I would have changed—they embarrass me to this day—but I relaxed and grew to believe that this was good work done well. I didn't trust it was my best, but I trusted the process I used to make it.

•••

It was mothering that saved me from the idea of doing my best, which is not exactly the same as perfectionism, but they are sisters wearing matching dresses. An hour or two into mothering, I knew it wouldn't always be pretty. On some days, good enough and "We are all now in bed" was a victory. We could begin again in the morning. I would learn to trust this process too, of loving and growing people despite not really knowing what I was doing.

As our three children became adults, so beautiful and complicated, my memories of the things I had done and the things I had left undone sometimes showed up, and demanded to be let in. It's hard to get memories out of the living room once they decide to take a seat. Every honest parent tangles with regrets. I know there are those who can briskly say, "Well Chloe, I did my best." I cannot honestly say I always did my best, as much as I would love to think that was even possible.

When I hear it, "I did my best," sounds like an excuse. When I say it, "I did my best" sounds like a weak apology. What we need to do in parenting and in writing—instead of our impossible best—is to do our work over and over again, and don't you dare give up. There will be sorrow and success and it's all a big stew on the stove. Forget about the best, in home and in art. Set that burden down, right at your weird-looking feet. Show up and try hard. That's how we help nurture people and poems. Trust the process more and trust our best less.

•••

This is very Anglican of us, this idea that process matters more than performance—that the way we make something has an important weight and is worthy of our trust. That when we do the same thing over and over again, we are training ourselves; and when a long time has passed, we find we will be better.

When we step into church and offer our sad and suspicious selves into the sacred sentences of worship, this is a deep relinquishment of trying to be our best. To trust the process in writing, or artmaking of any kind I am sure, is to believe in a liturgy of making that is true no matter how we feel on that day, it is scaffolding to scramble up to reach the higher places.

Daily Rituals: How Artists Work by Mason Currey provides a glimpse into the creative working lives of 161 artists of all kinds, and the "daily rituals to get done the work they love to do." My beloved short-story artist Alice Munro wrote, at the beginning at least, during her children's nap times, and then later when they were in school. Thomas Mann was always in his study by 9:00 a.m., where he wrote undisturbed until noon. My favorite might be choreographer George Balanchine, who planned and created while he ironed his clothing, almost daily. Ironing was a part of his process. He trusted the ironing. All the processes were different and fine-tuned and hard earned. These highly creative and accomplished writers, artists, musicians, and super-smart math people all discovered how to do good work well within the possibilities of their own lives. And then, they hit repeat (and tweaked occasionally, of course).

The process I trust is read, think, outline, walk, read, walk, despair, write, regret, write, leave in a warm place to let rise, and then revise again and again and again (as many times as time allows until I believe it is good enough. Revision is everything.), finish, send, be weird and go into sent folder to read email, see ridiculous error, email editor again almost immediately.

This process works for me, again and again. I know it and I trust it, although there are parts of it that I always hate. If I don't abandon process, I know that when I start at read, I will finish at emailing my editor twice in a row. I believe in this.

At the heart of our best work is not doing our best at all. It is showing up and working the process like my dog with his bone in our tiny backyard. Someday, at the end of our wild and creative lives when we hug our people goodbye and we have set down our paint and our pens for this time and place, maybe then there will be something beautiful we hold in our hands and say, "This is the best I did." I will wait.

Karen Stiller
Writer & Editor

PRYING OPEN OUR EYELIDS

Lauren Bentley

Did you see...? Did you see...?[3]

I HAVE BEEN A CHRISTIAN since before I was born. In summary: white, millennial, Evangelical, American expat in Canada. Roughly every five years, I have a terrible crisis of faith. Perhaps it's the exhaustion that comes from one too many news stories of the antics of my compatriots in my home country; or the friendly Canadian disdain for religious fervor; or too much divine silence; or too much noise of everything else.

Regardless, every five years, I am torn in two. I can't look at the glorious mountains edging my city or a dappled leaf fallen artfully on the lawn without despair. Am I seeing a world charged with God's grandeur? Or...happenstance? It's such a classic existential dilemma I'm embarrassed to be so cliché (again, millennial). Suddenly, everything I see turns into a question mark, like a cartoon in which a starving person starts seeing people with turkeys for heads. It's unbearable. I look to classic arguments about the existence of altruism; I consider determinism and its incalculable ramifications. If the pattern holds, in about a year I will come out of the crisis—the news

---

3   The questions in italics throughout are taken from Annie Dillard's essay collection, *The Abundance*, which includes excerpts from more than four decades of her writing.

will calm down, or God will show up, like an old friend driving unexpectedly into town on a motorcycle—and I will still have faith. But it will be reshaped, less clear, more worn at the edges by observing the world around me and being surprised, once again, at how untidy it can be.

•••

When I have spent my brain attempting to answer my own questions, I let Annie Dillard ask me hers. She has a way of prying open eyelids that isn't entirely unpleasant. For example:

Why do we people in churches seem like cheerful,
    brainless tourists on a packaged tour of the Absolute?

Is beauty itself an intricately fashioned lure,
    the cruelest hoax of all?

Why does death so catch us by surprise, and why love?

Would I eat a frog's leg if offered?

Why is there sand in deserts?

(And, for good measure:)

How?

Annie looks at gratuitous roses. She sees Orion arching, ready to pierce. She contemplates waterbugs and weasels and emptied frog bodies. After all her inquisition, I still have one question of my own: how much can I trust my own eyes?

In order to attract a mate, the Japanese pufferfish works for a week, without rest, to create an ornate monastic labyrinth at the bottom of the sea. He beats his body into the sand, into the act of creation, out-acting the current that threatens to sweep it all away. I watch a video of the phenomenon some kind soul has

posted online, eyes wide. When the fish goes so far as to deco-
rate the ridges with shells, I do cry, just a little. The camera pans
out on the intricate, perfect maze, edges lined with seashells,
all created where the light hardly shines. It is either the most
spectacular argument for divine existence (beauty requires a
witness) or the extent of the absurd (all this, for the dull-eyed
female) I've ever seen.

Is this beauty, these gratuitous roses, or a mere display of force?

Annie too seems to have an uneasy relationship with sight.
She demands it, constantly, almost overwhelmingly. Many
budding essayists I'm sure have been beleaguered by the idea
that they might be missing something imbued with great meaning after reading *Pilgrim at Tinker Creek*—the angle of a leaf in
relation to the light, perhaps, or the specific pattern a waterbug
makes on an otherwise still pond.

How many days have I learned not to stare at the back
  of my hand when I could be looking out at the creek?

She is, in fact, relentless. But she has no patience for funda-
mentalism: for the certainty of the eyes.

Does anyone have the foggiest idea what sort of power
  we so blithely invoke?

•••

Last night, Orion vaulted and spread all over the sky,
  pagan and lunatic, his shoulder and knee on fire,
  his sword three suns at the ready—for what?

Meanwhile, down here, I put my daughter in the bath. I dump
water on her hair from a small yellow bucket that looks like a
bee while she chews on one of her older brother's bath toys. I

stay in case she falls. My knees are wet, as are my arms up to elbows and many portions of my shirt. (More dappled things.) She lives for the bath. When I bring her into the bathroom for any other purpose, she lunges from my arms and whines, willing her small body into the tub. To get the same enjoyment from a water splash, an adult would need to river raft during the spring thaw.

How long, I wondered, could you stretch this out?

I wrap her in a mint green towel with a hood that looks like a bear. All good things must end, or maybe they go on for eternity. To live in a world where either one is plausibly true makes me hold on to her harder and wonder what I'll teach her about pleasure, love, duty, faith, and suffering. And if I will figure out any answers before she starts learning anyway.

She, my daughter, does teach me about joy, the thing small children are uniquely capable of illuminating for tired grown-ups. She invites me to share in her pleasure, and I feel gratitude toward this small thing I got to be part of creating. It was C.S. Lewis who said we couldn't fully feel a pleasure until it was shared with another. Picture this: God, outside of time, waits (a paradox). At night, he lies back on his cloudy bed and fondly looks forward to the time when humans create the underwater camera. He smiles, almost giddy, looking forward to the moment when his joy will be shared. "You guys have *got* to see this pufferfish!"

How boldly could you push an audience...to
*   please them in some way?*

Then again, maybe he doesn't. In which case:

Why should I open my eyes?

•••

Most human eyes have three color-receptor cones. A butterfly eye has four, as does a goldfish eye and in rare cases, a woman's. These tetrachromats see the world infused with colors most of us will never be able to perceive (this clandestine world of color is thought to be universally hidden from men).

Is this what we live for?

While Annie encourages us to look, to keep looking, interrogating with her endless questions (so often rhetorical), it's humbling to consider our deep inability to perceive the *allness* of anything. We have eyes, but though seeing, so often we cannot see.

After every crisis of faith, I find myself even more in the middle of knowing, existing between the poles of certainty. Simone Weil defines saintliness as "balance that leans both ways at once," but I'm still not comfortable in this in-between space where faith is less of a solid, stone monument to belief that may suffer erosion but never destruction. For many years, I thought it was realistic, holy even, to climb that monument until my head was above the clouds. Ironically, faith to me meant seeing everything, all at once.

No, in this space, faith is a gauzy veil that lets in much light but embraces some level of obfuscation. There is some risk here; it doesn't leave the door for doubt merely cracked. It throws it wide open to questions, some posed in my own mind, some gracefully penned by iconoclast essayists who get a thrill from interrogation. But I have come to believe that risk is a necessary condition for magic.

Why knock yourself out describing a dream?

Magic, as I define it for this essay: Experiencing the present with all the benefits of it being past. Hear me out. Not "living in the moment" with only thoughts of the present, as too many people require; but living in a moment while already appreciating the resonance it will have on your future—eternal or otherwise. A magic moment is one where you experience the present with an immediate, intrinsic understanding of its grandness, its meaning, without the mediation of reflection or memory.

The last year they allowed Halloween fireworks in Vancouver (a tradition, as far as I can tell, unique to British Columbia), I put my pirate-dressed four-year-old son in his car seat and drove the two blocks to Gray's Park. It is already dark at 7 p.m., the beginning of that time of year when you have to remind yourself to be awake.

We park across the street and run to the park holding hands, no cars on the road, just clusters of costumed families. We stand at the edge of the abandoned lawn bowling club, when suddenly the dark park is lit from within and the sky explodes. What can I say? It's fireworks (*the expensive ones,* I can hear my frugal mom saying in my head). We all know how they make our hearts explode too.

The City has banned fireworks in Vancouver starting November 1, so people are really going all out. It is the year of the pandemic, of massive wildfires that a month before had choked us with smoke, of political unrest and astronomical gun sales and the horror of I-Can't-Breathe, and people seem desperate to redeem this fire, to blow something up with gleeful purpose. To charge the sky with grandeur.

Was this not grand?

We'd already gone up and down the street once to trick-or-treat, many more houses dark this year but a few offering candy via PVC pipes taped to handrails, individual bags set out on self-serve tables, and cups on walkways lit by Jack-o-lanterns. The ones who celebrate really *celebrate*. I am grateful for these life-livers, these creative minds who put in the extra effort for four-year-old pirates who don't have any idea how strange this year of their childhood is.

The next day, we will learn about the half-a-million dollars in damage across the city, burned shingles, obscene litter. And yet, there is magic here, neighbors coming together, this collective dedication to creating bright bursts of joy.

What else can you risk with all your might but your life?

A week later, I read my son a children's book, *The Last Stop on Market Street*, by Matt de la Peña. A grandmother, Nana, takes her grandson on the bus, saying, "Boy, what do we need a car for?" Her goal is to teach him to witness their city in its darkness and light, not zoom past it blind.

To what end?

It reminds me of John Steinbeck in *Travels with Charley*, his 1960s travelogue about driving across America in his camper, Rocinante, eschewing the then-new interstate system for 30-mile-per-hour back roads. When I read *Travels with Charley* in my late teens, the thought of creeping across those 10,000 miles in a camper with a poodle filled me with dread. Nana would disagree.

As they ride down Market Street, a blind man gets on the bus.

"Nana, how come that man can't see?" the boy asks.

"What do you know about seeing? Some people watch the world with their ears," Nana replies.

Across the aisle, a guitarist begins to play. The blind man leans over to the grandmother and whispers, "To feel the magic of the music, I like to close my eyes."

When the music was going, who could resist?

•••

When I find myself in the middle part of faith, or of knowing, I long less for answers and more for peace. Annie's questions provide a level of comfort as my raft drifts away from the poles of certainty. At the very least, she offers a commitment to the act itself—a hope that comes from knowing questions are worth asking in the first place. Here's one more, my favorite:

Quick! Why aren't you dusting?

Dusting is an act of faith, in the same vein as giving birth to another human, brushing one's teeth, and owning a lawn mower. Annie does indeed offer an answer to this one: we, the dust-to-dust, dust to forestall burial. Dusting is an act that says there is a reason to pursue order in the chaos. In that way, every human, or most every I suppose, is a person of faith. We act as our answer to the questions of life. We dust anyways.

What else is there, or was there, or will there ever be?

Lauren Bentley
Writer & Editor

WRITING WITHIN & WITHOUT A COMMUNITY

Shonette Reed

MY GREATEST WINS and moments of success have come when I am grounded in community. From the nudge to enter an art or writing contest, to celebrating a placement, or even making it to the final round, it is a profound experience to be encouraged to move forward with a goal that visibly lights my entire face up. Community, in essence, is where I have thrived and grown into the person and creative I desire to be. It is an innate desire that God has placed in each of us, all the way from the beginning of creation.

When I started college in 2010, I had no intention of pursuing a journalism degree. Though I had started writing at the age of 9 in an after-school program, I kept most of it private—only sharing bits and pieces with those closest to me. But God, who made a point to speak to me through the voice of others, had a different plan. Whether it was an elementary school teacher who saw something in my poetry, a high school teacher who said I had a "strong voice" before I ever knew what voice was, or my freshmen seminar college professor who pointed out the skill in an assignment. This is where my safety began. But in college, I encountered a world where my safety began to shatter.

•••

I did not have a writing community in college. Whether it was school, an internship, or the journalism study-abroad program, finding community in other writers was far more difficult than it should have been. In time, I found it even more difficult to navigate school in the midst of other writers—whether it was in the criticism of the stories I wanted to tell, the lack of willingness to listen to students of color on campus who were not seen as valid, or the unreciprocated effort I found when I offered to lend an extra eye to someone else's work.

Whenever I made the attempt, there was always something that made writing—an activity I enjoyed and considered to be a communal effort—isolating. It felt like every corner I turned, there was another competition to gear up for. The lack of camaraderie nearly made me leave the world of media and publishing before I crossed the stage and received my degree. Having jobs at well-known publications was often held in high regard—yet, most of the time, as a Black woman, the faces that represented those well-known publications that my Christian college brought in to speak, weren't Black. It's not as though publications that catered to me did not exist, so why were they seemingly viewed as less than?

And while I don't think people meant harm, at times, I do know that there are systems in place to put writers in a position of running a rat race and seeing one another as competition over supporters and allies. I know that systems are in place to view one publication as higher than the other. And while, yes, there are spaces that are more credible than others, students came willing and ready to learn. Not to be overlooked and treated poorly if their work did not reflect what often catered to whiteness or a White standard. Not to be viewed as less than if their dream publication wasn't one that the masses clapped for.

These experiences hurt my view of the writing community. Competition took the place of community. If you were a journalism major with an emphasis in writing and publishing like I was, it was often looked down on because "print is dead." And, yet, little glimmers of hope made their way in. Every so often, someone from a different section of the journalism department would care to lend a hand—but these moments were few and far between. That should have never been.

As the luminous writer bell hooks revealed, "The intellectual tradition of the West is very individualistic. It's not community-based. The intellectual is often thought of as a person who is alone and cut off from the world. So I have had to practice being willing to leave the space of my study to be in community, to work in community, and to be changed by community." Writing was a solitary act. And while I do need quiet to tap into what I'm thinking, what I'm feeling, it's important for me to be able to break out and converse with other writers when I am too close to the work.

After graduation, I was able to do freelance work as I also worked a full-time, overnight job. It was in these spaces, holding different freelance positions, that I finally found a thriving writing community. Where writers championed one another and congratulated each other on accomplishments, even while small. And through that, I began to care about writing again.

I noticed this trend as I carried on in smaller communities doing good work after college. I learned that there are people who want to help. There are people who want to see other writers win, even if it's before them. Or as Kendrick Lamar says, *"I wanna see all my dogs make it. Even if it's before me."* And through this, I've moved from labeling myself as simply a journalist or writer—though both are important and dear to me.

•••

It's amazing the ways you begin to view yourself and your work when you can exist in safe spaces. Creating spaces that we have not seen before is difficult, but it is not impossible. We see time and time again throughout scripture when God calls someone to a mission and equips them in a way to move forward. Whether these biblical individuals find excuses to hesitate based on their fear, anger, or doubt, they eventually gain the courage and ability as the call of God and the desires of their heart align with Christ as the ultimate importance.

To state the obvious, community starts with creation in Genesis 1. Yet, the creation of spaces where people are free to exist, discover, and flourish together is not an easy feat. America has a system in place that has been entrenched over 400 years that has thrived off pushing down one group while uplifting another. Yet, as we question why we hold to certain things, and as we fight for equity—having people at tables who are able to speak and shed light at these tables—I believe we will prevail.

•••

Through my time in post-grad life, I have found myself constantly challenged by what I read and who I engage with to create the world I want to see. It is easy to become weighed down by what is, that we forget what can be. Throughout this journey, the work of bell hooks reminds me once again, *"To build community requires vigilant awareness of the work we just continually do to undermine all the socialization that leads to behave in ways that perpetuate domination."*

I don't expect every space to be a mixture of all people. There are times when spaces both need and deserve to be more exclusive, especially as we live in a world that shows just how deeply White supremacy is rooted in our society—sometimes, one simply needs the space to breathe.

My journey to writing, to building my own community of creatives, has been a constant state of trial and error. No one gets it right the first time, but we must fight toward a world that honors people over productivity and praises the people themselves, over the work we deem to be worthy of a hand-clap.

I do, for some reason, have hope that this will come. I have lived it. And while I may not see it perfected in my lifetime, both myself, and those I've chosen to surround myself with, can honor the future by doing the work now.

Shonette Reed

Writer & Editor

CRAFT

HOLY WEIRDNESS

Josh Tiessen

...I saw the Lord, high and exalted, seated on a throne; and the train of his robe filled the temple. Above him were seraphim, each with six wings: With two wings they covered their faces, with two they covered their feet, and with two they were flying. And they were calling to one another: "Holy, holy, holy is the Lord Almighty; the whole earth is full of his glory." At the sound of their voices the doorposts and thresholds shook and the temple was filled with smoke.

Isaiah 6:1-4 NIV

I DESCEND FROM A HOLY HERITAGE of Christian martyrs, pastors, and missionaries who dedicated their lives to serving the Lord and ministering to people. I was born in Moscow, Russia, to Canadian parents who taught at a Christian university, training young pastors for ministry in a country healing from the brutality of atheistic communism. From as young as I can remember, I believed in God and wrestled with the big questions of life. As I grew older my faith matured, and I sought to follow the way of Jesus with faithfulness.

I developed an artistic flair from the time I could hold a fat crayon in my little hand, spending long hours as a preschooler doing crafts with my Russian nanny. I requested stylish clothes and unusual haircuts—from the colored spiky-do of the early 2000s to the emo side-sweep of the 2010s. While friends bragged about their latest video game conquests on Halo, I quietly studied under a pet portrait artist who helped me stage my first fine art exhibition at the age of eleven. That Easter, instead of a chocolate bunny, I asked for *The Passion of the Christ.* I guess you could say I was an odd little duck.

My parents were not artists, but I was fortunate to fall down the rabbit hole into the art world by way of the wildlife art scene in Canada. By invitation, I was mentored at fifteen under the world's most well-known wildlife artist, Robert Bateman. During this mentorship, I studied alongside a few Christian artists, who were some of the kindest and most supportive people I knew. In the following years, I frequently met Jesus-followers at regional art festivals. Throughout the United States at juried gallery shows I met accomplished artists of faith exhibiting traditional representational art.

By my late teens, I had found my own artistic voice and transitioned away from naturalistic wildlife art. I began juxtaposing animals in abandoned ruins, lacing my paintings with stories and symbolism. I called my style "narrative hyper-surrealism." While my new work was accepted into contemporary avant-garde galleries in New York City, Los Angeles, and Portland, a new observation dawned on me: all the Christians had disappeared.

•••

I have often been perplexed by the reality that though the Bible is chock-full with strange tales of talking snakes, seraphim covered in eyes from wing-to-wing, and dead men coming to life, most of the last century of Christian art is tame, predictable, and palatable. As for music, I wonder if anyone else has grown weary from the proliferation of worship songs with clichés about breaking chains, or the never-ending references to water. It's easy to poke fun at kitsch-y Thomas Kinkade cottage landscapes and Greg Olsen biblical prints found in your local Christian bookstore. But in a different way this is also present in the millennial Christian culture, where the creative output is kinfolk-style minimalism with Bible verses overlaying pastel tones. We merely replaced the sentimental with the slick.

I get it. In the hopes of making Christianity "seeker sensitive," we want to present our faith in an accessible way—so we draw on safe themes for art and music, like purpose, freedom, and comfort, which resonate with the largely suburban culture in which our churches are located. The nagging question is: are we being dishonest and doing society a disservice by covering up the "holy weirdness" of our faith? While many churches in the West have attempted to make the ancient religion of Christianity more normal and relevant in order to appease a secular audience, trends now indicate that our culture is actually doing the reverse. The cool logic of naturalistic materialism is giving way to a tsunami of interest in the esoteric world of New Age. I have seen this most evidently in my artist colleagues who regularly incorporate indigenous spirituality, psychedelic, and shamanist themes into their art. Maybe it's time for us to rediscover and embrace the "holy weirdness" of Christianity.

•••

In my escapades through art history, I've found many artists of faith who have integrated the wild and wonderful in their work. Perhaps we can look to them as guides, or at least conversational partners as we aim to reconcile an ancient faith with a postmodern world.

What I find fascinating is the kind of art that my non-Christian artist friends are attracted to—whether that be mysterious Byzantine icons or the organic whimsy of Antoni Gaudí's *Sagrada Família* cathedral.

One of the most popular works, especially among surrealist painters, is Hieronymous Bosch's *The Garden of Earthly Delights* (1495-1505). If you have not done so already, take a moment to gaze at this iconic triptych and notice your visceral reaction. Are you intrigued, repulsed, confused?

At first glance, you might think this eccentric artist must have indulged in magic mushrooms, with all his bizarre and fantastical creatures. However, Bosch descended from a family of painters who were members of the Illustrious Brotherhood of our Blessed Lady, a conservative religious group that held to Christian belief and overtly critiqued the lavishness of the Catholic Church. According to historian Terry Glaspey, in his book *75 Masterpieces Every Christian Should Know,* Bosch himself had a great familiarity with the Bible and wished to convey the reality of sin, judgment, and hell.

The meaning of *The Garden of Earthly Delights* is debated, but with the artist's Christian context in mind it is not so challenging to decipher. The first panel presents the Garden of Eden, in which the Lord is communing with Adam and Eve (Genesis 3:8) showing the initial harmony enjoyed between nature, humans, and their Creator. The second panel depicts The Fall—humans multiply and fill the earth (Genesis 1:28), sin enters the world (Genesis 3), then humanity devolves into wickedness and indulgence (Genesis 6:5). The third panel projects the theme of apocalyptic judgment—sinful humanity left to its own devices turns chaotic and leads to self-destruction. While God's holy judgment will be for the unredeemed who have followed their sinful nature, for the godly it will be a joyous occasion of God laying bare the earth in order to purify it for the New Creation (2 Peter 3:10-13).

A couple years ago, I was sitting in a friend's living room surrounded by a pleasant group of Christian artists sipping tea and nibbling on biscuits. I thought it was the perfect time to express my appreciation for Bosch and his faith-filled work. To my dismay, I was met with disdain and apathy for this Early Netherlandish master.

What Christians fail to recognize is that Bosch created his own vocabulary of symbols, which many years later inspired fantasy and surrealist artists attracted to his aesthetic, inventing ghoulish creatures and imaginative worlds. However, unlike the fantasy genre which is often purely for entertainment value, Bosch used vivid metaphors for holy purposes to warn of the easy path toward self-indulgence.

•••

Perhaps even more undervalued by Christians are the mystical saints of the Church, such as the 12th century Benedictine abbess and polymath Hildegard of Bingen. With a deep respect for the Creator and creation, she was the first to study natural science in Germany with her work *Physica* and *Causae et Curae*. Like the mystical female artisan of Proverbs 8 delighting in creation, Hildegard loved music and pioneered the first musical, allowing nuns under her care to perform moral plays, even letting down their hair and wearing colorful dresses. She experienced multiple visions throughout her life, recording them in her theological volume, *Scivias*. She also directed artistic illuminations to bring her unusual visions to life, depicting themes of creation, incarnation, the new heavens and the new earth, combining these with Eastern mandala motifs in vibrant hues.

While Hildegard was almost lost to the sands of time, her life and work has been re-discovered. What made her *weird* in her day, namely being a female theologian and nature mystic, is now intriguing. Through her writings, she has helped contemporary Christians reconnect to the feminine aspects of embodied living and the sacredness of nature. Yet, Hildegard was far from a fourth-wave feminist or syncretistic nature-worshiper, showing that outliers can be sincere followers of Christ and remain theologically orthodox.

The influence of Christian mystics has endured over the years. In fact, while many modern artists of the 19th-20th centuries eschewed organized religion, those interested in faith often drew from the mystical tradition. (My colleagues William Dyrness and Jonathan Anderson have catalogued this in their book, *Modern Art and the Life of a Culture.*) One of these artists was the surrealist painter Salvador Dalí. While best known for his wild lifestyle and dream-inspired paintings of melting clocks and whimsical figures, he was also drawn to the visions of St. John of the Cross. According to historian Matthew Milliner's "Artists Gone Mild" Tower Talk, an entire catechesis can be taught based on Dalí's works of the incarnation, eucharist, crucifixion, and ascension. While visiting the National Gallery of Art in Washington, DC, many years ago, I was surprised to encounter a monumental painting by Dalí of the *Last Supper,* adorned with his mystical hallmarks.

•••

Alongside my full-time work as a professional artist from the time I was sixteen, I studied very part-time toward a Bachelor of Religious Education degree in Arts and Biblical Studies, taking me nine years to complete. While I cherished the time with my professors and was thoroughly enriched by the high quality education I received, I struggled most with classes on the Bible. I was troubled by the 19th-20th century form critics who sought to "demythologize" Scripture. They claimed that anything supernatural was simply a later addition, and that when you looked "behind the text" only the natural remained. For a season I experienced great consternation when reading the Bible. Were the critics right? Was the Bible just a work of legend from a pre-scientific age?

Around that time, I discovered the Bible Project, a series of animated videos on YouTube explaining biblical books and key themes. They approach Scripture on its own terms, as both fine literary art and divine inspiration. They admit it's weird, in fact "holy weird" (I recommend their trippy "Spiritual Beings" video series, a careful and imaginative exegesis of the ancient supernatural worldview that inspired Scripture). The co-founder, Dr. Tim Mackie, is the only PhD I know of who skateboards to work. Curiously, the Bible Project is based in Portland, Oregon, known for its idiosyncratic blend of weirdness and post-Christian culture. The Bible Project spoke to me as an artist and intellectual, and helped rehabilitate my love for the Bible. I am heartened that "holy weirdness" is being embraced by some Christian artists and thinkers of our day.

•••

. I recently attended a megachurch for a few years, where I experienced a sub-culture in which sharing doubts and grappling with questions was discouraged, preferring cookie-cutter Christians who give pat answers and pray predictable prayers. Not surprisingly, I found few artists there. Great art doesn't flourish in a culture of creative and theological homogeneity. Embracing the weirdness of our faith through art can be disarming for people who generally think religious art (not to mention evangelism) is about selling something that comprises propositional truths which cannot be questioned.

As I alluded to earlier, in my subject matter as a hyper-surrealist oil painter, I often juxtapose animals into abandoned remnants of human civilizations, highlighting irony and parody, the hallmarks of postmodern art. This is best seen in my thematic body of work *Streams in the Wasteland* (2015-2021), inspired by nature's reclamation in the book of Isaiah. I write about why my work has been accepted in the mainstream art world in spite of the fact that it draws upon biblical and theological themes. In my recently published art monograph *Streams in the Wasteland,* the final painting in the series, *Agnus Dei,* was inspired by the Lamb of God symbolism in Isaiah 53, echoed in Revelation 5, where all the creatures on earth and in the sea encircle the throne, praising the Lamb who was slain. Curiously, animals seldom appear in Western (Christian) art, despite a plethora of biblical references. I suspect it is because an interest in animals has been seen as childish, reminiscent of children's storybooks and antithetical to grown-up, sanitized Christianity. However, as Balaam's donkey did, could creation itself jolt us to turn to our mysterious Creator? (Numbers 22:21-39).

The value of humor and irony in the current cultural ethos finds its roots in the writings of the Christian existentialist philosopher Søren Kierkegaard, who recognized that faith is filled with paradox and the "virtue of the absurd." Our culture has become wary of confrontational truth claims because of their associations with abuses of power at the hands of traditional religious institutions and political ideologues. As Mark Shaw writes in *Work, Play, Love,* "In the postmodern world the best way to subvert the pretensions of power is to mix and match form and content. The 'trivial' is freed to serve the truth, and the truth is liberated from the hands of the powerful or learned to partner with the playful to accomplish a common purpose."

In an age skeptical of objective universal truths, might an approach through art that infuses the strange, ironic, and humorous provide some levity for generally taboo subjects like the meaning of life and opposing belief systems? What might Christian communities miss if we sanitize the Bible, making it less weird? To me that seems dishonest, especially as I strive toward authenticity in my own work. Granted, there are risks in embracing a "holy weirdness"—we could be mocked or misunderstood, or we may be tempted to compromise theologically, trying to blend Christianity with Hindu, Buddhist, or the New Age iconography currently in vogue.

In order for "holy weirdness" to flourish, we need to be shaped by the totality of Scripture. According to *The New Bible Dictionary,* holiness refers to consecration of a person, day, or place for a divine purpose. While God is the paragon of holiness, as the perfect embodiment of ethical purity, He "disciplines us for our good, in order that *we may share in his holiness*" (Hebrews 12:10 NIV, emphasis added). In his teaching series "Future Church," John Mark Comer asserts that while the word *holy* sounds outdated, accruing shameful baggage for many people, it's too important a word to abandon. He goes on to say that in the New Testament the word for holy, *hagios,* means unique, special, or different, but can also be translated "weird." We must submit to living differently, in order that the art we make be likewise a participation in God's holiness. In addition to Scripture, we can look to mystical artists throughout church history like Hieronymous Bosch and Hildegard of Bingen, to guide us on our artistic journey. For accountability, it is important to be part of a local community of believers who not only affirm our gifting but are there to "reel us in" if needed.

While my proposal of "holy weirdness" may be risky, we are called to engage our generation in their native tongue of doubt and dialogue—prioritizing the dialectic over the dogmatic. The days of "easy Christianity" that blends into the culture are quickly passing by, and we are already perceived as weirdos in our society. The arts need not be the Church's public relations arm presenting a predictably sanitized faith. Rather, as artists press into the mystery of our ancient faith, we can trust God to use what the world may deem as "foolishness" to further his mission of redeeming culture for his glory (1 Corinthians 1:21).

Admittedly, I struggle on the lonely road of non-conformity to the monolithic Christian arts culture, and I puzzle as to why there are so few Christians in the contemporary art world. But I have come to realize that I am called to take the path less traveled, not unlike some of the historical artists mentioned above. To be sure, it is a solitary path and I often feel equally out of place in the Christian culture and the contemporary art world, with very little overlap in between. Perhaps "holy weirdness" is a bridge where both communities could meet. Contemporary artists of our day are already hanging out on the fringes, waiting for the Church to embrace an ancient-future aesthetic.

Josh Tiessen
Artist & Writer

TO BE A CHRISTIAN POET

D.S. Martin

TO BE A CHRISTIAN POET—or a poet who is a Christian, if you prefer—is to be a reconciler of contradictions. It is a vocation of being misunderstood and marginalized, where rewards are difficult to quantify, and even the purpose behind such a life is questioned, by all except a few visionaries—who may in turn be dismissed for celebrating something with little obvious pragmatic value.

Some callings of self-sacrifice are widely acknowledged as noble. I come from a family of missionaries. My mom grew up in China, the daughter of career missionaries; the oldest of four sisters, and the only one who didn't follow in the "family business." Such a focused calling would only be questioned outside Christian circles.

FINDING A FUTURE

When I was a kid, I would have loved to look into my future and see myself as anything. What was I good at? School was a wash-out. I wasn't disciplined, and I was very good at becoming distracted—a daydreamer, who lived in his own head. I enjoyed sports, but wasn't aggressive or especially skilled; I loved music, but was too impatient to endure practicing; I certainly didn't fit into the not-good-at-school category of being mechanical. I liked going to church—singing, stories, hanging out with friends—but I was not good at sitting still.

What I did learn early, was that the one place where an uncategorizable kid like me belonged was in the love of Jesus. I didn't have to deserve it. I didn't even have to be "well-behaved" in Sunday school—although I did try. I just had to give him my heart. It wasn't a difficult decision if you recognize what a one-sided exchange that was. And so, I quickly identified myself as a Christian.

Problem. If you are not the star of the classroom or the baseball diamond, it is not a confidence-building thing to see yourself as different from those around you. If you are already a keep-to-yourself person, it drives you further into an internal life. I became a thinker, a dreamer, a considerer of contradictions, but I didn't yet value my own intellect. I flourished in my own unremarkable way in our church community, becoming quite good at memorizing Bible verses, but I merely saw this as what you did, not as an accomplishment.

In contrast with this, I found delight, and connection with the outside world, through music. My church friends listened to secular music too, but for most it wasn't the obsession it became for me. To my parents' generation, this was not an acceptable passion for a good Christian boy, but the popular music of the '60s and '70s provided a banquet for the hunger of my internal life. Even so, it confirmed—at least in my mind—my place as an outsider even in the church.

THE POET'S ROVING EYE

All of this sounds like a recipe for failure. Even well into my years of persistent dedication to the art of poetry, it had not dawned on me what all this meant. One early clue was this quote from the Irish-British novelist Elizabeth Bowen:

> The writer, unlike his non-writing adult friend, has no predisposed outlook; he seldom observes deliberately. He sees what he did not intend to see; he remembers what does not seem wholly possible. Inattentive learner in the schoolroom of life, he keeps some faculty free to veer and wander. His is the roving eye.

The late great Canadian poet Margaret Avison touched on this too, in her poem "Poetry Is":

> Poetry is always in
>   unfamiliar territory.
>
> At a ballgame when
>   the hit most matters
>   and the crowd is half-standing
>   already hoarse, then poetry's
>   eye is astray to a
>   quiet area to find out
>   who picks up the bat the runner
>   flung out of his runway...

This was a revelation! They were both speaking about me. I had thought I had chosen poetry, but now I began to realize I had been made to be a poet. Being an auditory learner—which had helped me learn my memory verses—led to my love of music and the music of language. Being an evangelical baptized me in scripture—sitting under pastors who took very seriously every single word in a passage they were preaching from—attuned me to the linguistic precision that poetry requires. Even being an outsider was part of the plan.

All artists are outsiders. They are not those at the center of attention, but those observing—sometimes watching the athletes and class clowns, sometimes seeing the way wisps of cloud float across the sky. There are, of course, extroverted artists—the dancers, the actors, the orators—but true artists have something of the outsider deep inside.

BARRIERS TO ENTRY

I'm not saying that if you don't see yourself in my story that you can't become a Christian poet. I'm saying that often the things about ourselves that we would call God's mistakes, or our own shortcomings, are often the very things God uses to lead us to be who he has made us to be.

Even so, there are huge barriers for anyone who has been called by God to be a Christian artist. The whole idea goes against the evangelical grain.

- There's a pragmatic evangelism-is-all-that-matters mindset, despite the teaching of scripture about our primary purpose being giving glory to God.

- There's a value in the broader culture about working hard to earn money—the Protestant work ethic—which would consider art to only be suitable as a hobby.

- To write a poem is an incredibly audacious thing to do. Who are you to think that others should pay any attention to your art? Christians are called to humility, not pride.

- Ever since the Enlightenment there has been a belief that reason trumps imagination—as though only what is seen is to be believed. Church leaders who lack artistic expertise, are often suspicious of the arts, feeling they need to be in control of all sanctioned content.

The only reason to be a Christian artist is that God has called you to be a Christian artist. To not obey this calling, I believe, leads to a life of disappointment. Let me share a bit of my ongoing story.

A LIFETIME OF POETRY

This is a story of years—of reading the best poetry I can get my hands on, of writing poems, of submitting poems to journals, of having poems rejected, of revising, of praying, of the kindness of Christian poets who are further along the road than I am, of reading mountains of poetry, of tiny victories, of becoming a teacher and sharing my love of poetry with young students, of group critiques with writing friends, of reviewing music and poetry books, of dreaming and scheming and praying, of questioning myself over and over, of attending conferences, of writing, of revising, of submitting, of further rejection, of further revision, of more successes, of taking chances, of praying, of actually getting a chapbook of my poetry published, of having my first full-length book published, of beginning my blog *Kingdom Poets*, of beginning to teach poetry at conferences, of being invited to edit my own poetry series with Wipf & Stock Publishers (where I have now edited more than thirty books), of writing, of revising, of still facing the rejection of poems, of finding my place as a Christian poet, of researching, of praying, of reading the best Christian poetry I can find, of publishing poetry anthologies, of having poems appear in journals near and far, of creating ways to be an encourager and facilitator for Christian poets, of becoming Poet-in-Residence at McMaster Divinity College, of developing a writing technique of intense revision, of becoming friends with many of my favorite poets, of opportunities further-a-field to be the visiting poet, of being a dad and a husband and someone who loves to lead a small group with friends from church, of being an introvert who quietly does his own thing barely comprehended by friends, of becoming a grandfather in the midst of this Corona crisis, of being extremely content and thankful for the blessings of my life.

Every Christian artist must decide for herself to what extent her faith will appear in her work. I always told my students, "Poets write about things that matter," and so for me the decision was obvious. I had to write about spiritual things. Even when I am writing about something distinctly earth-bound, God tends to force his way into my observations.

Winnipeg poet Sarah Klassen says in her poem "Horizon":

It isn't easy writing a poem
    about Jesus. You could write the sun
    hung low over olive groves

...But his hard words
    his terrible naked mercy
    hang like an awkwardness
    across a gaunt horizon...

As I undertook my vocation, I hadn't planned to become such an encourager of other poets. For ten years now I have been profiling poets and their work on my blog *Kingdom Poets*. I write about today's best-known Christian poets, about those who are less known, about famous poets and not-so-famous poets of the past—highlighting those who speak profoundly of faith in God. I profile poets from around the world and from various denominational backgrounds. In doing this I magnify the legacy of those who have gone before, encourage today's readers to investigate their contributions, and celebrate the work of the poets who are writing today. I have also developed venues for Christian poetry to appear, such as my web-journal *Poems For Ephesians*, which is on the McMaster Divinity College website, and the three anthologies I have produced. This was God's plan, not mine.

As a poet, I have become a better reader of the Bible—comprehending the poetic veins that run from Genesis through Revelation. I have learned to better read between the lines of scripture, and between the lines of experience, as the Spirit communicates what must be perceived through the Spiritual imagination. I have learned, better than I otherwise would, how to walk with the unseen. To be a Christian poet is for me the best life I could ever dream.

D.S. Martin
Poet & Editor

TREASURES OF DARKNESS
On Image, Intuition, and the Christian Writer

Paul J. Pastor

And I will give thee the treasures of darkness,
and hidden riches of secret places...

Isaiah 45:3 KJV

IN THE FOREST BEHIND MY HOUSE (which perches delicately on the border of the unbroken woods that stretch south from the Columbia River into the Cascade mountains of Oregon), there are many dozens of red alder snags that sit, quite silently, in the shifting light.

If you walked through these woods, "Taking the route you would be likely to take / From the place you would be likely to come from," to quote Eliot, you would see these snags, standing dead and fairly unremarkable, scattered among Douglas firs and garryana oaks, the lower portions of their trunks obscured by sword ferns. The decaying alders would be pitted by woodpeckers, cherished by gray squirrels hoarding wild hazelnuts into their hollows. Perhaps you would see one where the bark has been shuffled down by a black bear, greedy for waxy grubs. But what you would not see, not unless you came with eyes to see and at the right time to see, would be the oysters.

Through the rain-soaked alders, the oyster mushroom, *Pleurotus ostreatus* (perhaps its close cousin, *pulmonarius*), one of nature's great hunters, is dancing. Through the colossal nutrient bank of the decaying wood, blooming with the myriad organisms that eat and rejoice, the mycelium of *Pleurotus* spreads—intelligent, hungry, and vigorous.

When we think of mushrooms, most of us think of what can be seen—the squamous, glabrous flutes, bulbs, and trumpets of the fungi that riot from wood or soil to briefly announce their alien presence before deflating into liquescence. But the part we see is to the creature merely what a cherry is to its tree—the fruit. The life of the thing lies deep and out of sight.

The true creature below the fleshy fruit—neither of kingdom Plantae nor of kingdom Animalia, but of kingdom Fungi—is an intelligent colony of living threads. It is something very much like roots, and something very much like the neural network of your brain, and a little more and a little less than either of those.

In the case of the oyster, the omnivorous mycelium is both devouring the wet wood of those red alders and actively hunting the tiny roundworms that fill it. Within minutes of contact, *Pleurotus* paralyzes the worm by sending a chemical message that tells its body to go into a premature rigor mortis, slips a tendril noose of itself around the prey, sends a filament through the mouth of the worm, and begins to digest it.

Then twice a year, for a month or more, the mycelium will fruit. In great flushes of shelved fungus (I have found some more than 14 inches wide growing far above my reach, which I popped loose with a forked hazel wand and caught in my hat), the wild hunter of the inner intimacies of the logs will burst into the light in edible bundles of pure nutrients and protein, loved alike by all from insects to poets. The pearlescent oysters are the stallions of the mushroom world, thick and fast and confident, able to climb within the dead snags to heights of thirty or forty feet over the course of only a few years, working to make wood into soil, to make worms into food, and living a remarkable life, at once vicious hunter and abundant gift, wise, fierce, and generous.

•••

I occupy the often awkward position (navigated before me by some of my favorite thinkers, including Charles Williams, T.S. Eliot, and Brian Doyle) of being both a professional editor and a working poet. In my experience, both good editing and decent poetry require a comfort with invisible work, and a sense of the importance of that invisible work. Both require a formidable, aggressive power of digestion. Both require a willingness, when ready, to "fruit," suddenly bringing the best gifts of slow, invisible processes into the light for others to eat. In that work (it is much like feeling one's way through a dark, nutritious log), I have found many treasures. While it is easy to bemoan the horribly commercialized state of modern publishing (particularly Christian publishing), there is much to love.

But I will also note that even among some of our tradition's best voices today, there is a near-total absence of two great spiritual and artistic treasures: *image* and *intuition.* Our writers seem almost wholly dependent on outside sources for these particular creative riches. Great things are quoted, from generations before, or from outside the Christian fold. We are no longer mining them ourselves, and we think of the resulting poverty as normal or natural for Christians. It is neither normal, nor natural. It should never become so.

We might think of creativity as a process of mining (or hunting) for good things: jewels, or pearls, or nutritious roundworms in the depths of a red alder. The better of our Christian writers today seem very well-equipped to get those treasures that are in the "light." These are rational treasures—clear arguments, good thought—and emotive treasures of depth of feeling and well-articulated loves. But there is so little being done to *dig* for what is hidden, for what is unseen (pardon the constant metaphor, I know no other way to speak of it), that it is not much of an exaggeration to say that it is not being done, or at least not being published. *Image* and *intuition* seem to have been forgotten as literary or spiritual treasures. The holy darkness is quiet beneath us, unbroken by the ring of picks or the glint even of a candle.

By *image* I mean something that includes *symbol, archetype,* and *icon,* but is more than each of those. I mean the raw stuff of which dreams are made. This is the native language of the deep soul, which speaks to itself exclusively in pictures. The artist who holds this jewel finds they have the ability to manipulate the web of images and forms that unites the human psyche with the natural world of creation and the relational world of humankind—both of which flow quite directly from the mind of the Creator. It is easier to describe the effects of *image* than to define it. The effects are of a kind of haunting—"pictures" that bleed from a story, painting, film, poem, etc., back into one's life. The mind returns to a complex image or set of images; finds itself wanting or needing to be inside them, to touch and interact with them. These images are multifaceted, magnetic, inherently interesting, and capable of sustaining long attention, continuing to reveal gifts for a very long time. Dream-stuff. Icon-stuff.

By *intuition* I mean a process of "gut-knowing" that we have rejected, dismissed, and generally talked ourselves out of (as a Western culture and as Christians) largely since the Medieval period darkened into the Enlightenment. One can tell a culture's health in this area by the level of importance it places upon dreams. Once nearly universally regarded as a source of unconscious and numinous insight, our society treats dreams like they treat the organ meat of the animals we slaughter—as garbage. This despite the fact that many traditional cultures, in exceptional wisdom, view the organs of an animal as precious and powerful, a choice delicacy!

But us? We do not like the guts. We are not used to the guts. They contain odd flaps. They are floppy and smell of copper. We are not willing even to sample them. We throw our dreams away; we cannot stomach the taste. They make us nervous. (We know, after all, that the gut is what inevitably holds those good and brutal truths the mind refuses.)

Image and intuition—the "gut" element of creativity—seem to have become spiritual and artistic treasures that Christian writers today cannot (or do not) intentionally or skillfully access. And yet, they are among our heritage, both as humans and as Christians. Both seem foreign to us. They are ours by birthright, but we have lost them. We might read the image-work of the prophet Ezekiel:

> *"The hand of the Lord was upon me, and carried me out in the spirit of the Lord, and set me down in the midst of the valley which was full of bones";*

or the apostle John:

> *"To him that overcometh will I give to eat of the hidden manna, and will give him a white stone, and in the stone a new name written, which no man knoweth saving he that receiveth it";*

or St. Julian of Norwich in her *Showings:*

> *"And in this he showed me a little thing, the quantity of a hazel nut, lying in the palm of my hand";*

or more modern masters (George MacDonald chief among them), but the thing awake in them to see such things and write of them seems asleep in us. The images enlighten us, but only from the outside, like lanterns held by a foreign hand.

One could object that the three examples I have just cited are, explicitly, *revealed* examples; that there is a spiritual aspect to them that is not easily replicated, and that ought not to be attempted for means of creative expression. But could not the same be said of the psalmist's emotive poetry, or of the apostle Paul's intricate logical discourses, both of which are accessed and imitated without hesitation by worship songwriters and preachers every weekend? If the gifts of feeling and thinking can be so mined for fresh work today, why not those of even deeper wells, the intuitive? Why not the exceptional power of the distilled image? This is part of the reason the treasures have become lost: we are not bold enough to even look for them. It is easier to dismiss, to stay in the cold light, rather than to seek Isaiah's "hidden riches."

To be fair, very few artists today of any kind, Christian or not, do this honestly or well. The filmmaker David Lynch is one of the few who come to mind from the contemporary scene, but he is enough to indicate what I mean. To watch a Lynch creation is often described as "weird" or "dreamlike." But there is a *logic* to it. There is an internal self-consistency that convinces the viewer that they are in the presence of something large and beautifully intricate, whose colors, forms, and movements are all communicating something to a level deeper than our rational mind. I cannot think of any significant Christian writers today who do this. We have many writing (or attempting to write) in the traditions of Annie Dillard, Wendell Berry, or James Baldwin. We have none today working in the traditions of Robert Bly, Shirley Jackson, Paul Claudel, or Haruki Murakami. (I exclude myself as I am not successful enough to be significant at the time of this writing. Please immediately buy many copies of my books.) This could be unfairly bleak, and I admit that I have not read *all* the books. But I believe that it is true, or nearly so.

•••

My sincere hope and my creative vision is that the rich thinking and deep emotion that characterize the best writing today—including the best writing by Christians—may be balanced by a rediscovery of the dream-thing, the image-thing in us. To recover this will be a process that involves dedication to an overlooked aspect of the creative-writing craft: that of the digestion of rich, complex images and the ability to, sometimes, do by not-doing, create by not-creating. We must commit ourselves to practices of digestion, learning to hunt like the oyster, to reclaim the inner state of more "primitive" (the word is backwards and yet true) humanity, who would starve the body at times of spiritual need to better encourage the coming of deep dreams.

The human psyche has been made by God to eat and hunt images, to intuit its way through the world as a pattern-making creature. The Christian tradition, in the long view, has remarkable resources for the writer and the artist to fuel these patterns. Our faith's most rooted Way holds the natural world in great regard as a place of embodied spirituality and immanent meaning.

Our prophets and mystics point us to the spiritual and aesthetic beauty of our visions, night-time dreams, reveries, and interactions with the rich symbol and spiritual depth of natural and human images. Following the example of the apostle Paul, we are able to welcome the cultural riches of other traditions—including the wealth of world myth, literature, and folktale—with a generous orthodoxy able to "chew the meat and spit the bones," rather than calcifying into small parochialisms. In all this, we can affirm the "treasures of darkness," and ground ourselves in pursuit of the soulful, the deep and the quiet, in the hidden riches of the world and of our own lives. We can hunt our dreams within the rich, damp logs of our lives. We can learn to write and work with intuitive, emotive, and rational skill, moving creatively from the gut through the heart and out the brain.

Should we be brave and humble enough to do the work of secret digestion, to hunt out and be hunted by the dream-stuff, it is my belief that we will put ourselves in the way of great work to come. Should we be able to reclaim this, to learn from the oddnesses of the oyster's secret hunt, I believe that we will find ourselves in the presence of a new set of quite wonderful creative problems. For rather than the hollowness and thin veneer of so much of our writing—so much of even our very good writing—we will find ourselves routinely in the company of vast and mighty presences: images that move like behemoths in the light-dappled forests of our souls; images that we may approach and tame in the name of Christ, upon which we may ride to far horizons.

Paul J. Pastor
Writer & Editor

THE IRRESISTIBLE PERIL OF PUBLISHING

Sara Billups

LATE ONE NIGHT MANY YEARS AGO, my infant son started to cry and couldn't be consoled. An hour passed, and nothing else worked to calm him, we got in the car and started driving. We drove east through cornfields and toward a circular cloud with a thunderstorm inside. A storm contained in a floating orb, a cumulonimbus with lightning shooting through its veins like an aorta or an electric eel. My son had long since stopped crying, but we kept moving toward the cloud.

Sometimes, writing has the same pull. It's often a drag, always a practice, but those of us who write or do any kind of creative work are often moving toward a hovering story that's always a little more east, a few miles further ahead.

Somewhere along the way, many of us think about writing a book.

To secure a traditional book deal in 2020, it doesn't matter if you are the next Denise Levertov or Anne Lamott, if you don't have a hearty Instagram following. Publishing is a business, and regardless of whether or not you or your agent pitches a big 5

New York house or a traditional faith-based publisher, the same industry truth applies: books are made to be sold.

Staff at Christian publishers may pray before an acquisitions meeting, but in an era when Christian bookstores are closing and belts are tightening, at the end of the day book contracts typically go to people who will sell the most books. On the other hand, major secular houses and small literary presses are less likely to publish work from folks writing from a clear Christian perspective. To identify as a Christian and write a book for a New York house, here is your best shot: expose a part of the church that's broken, then slip in at the end that you're a person of faith, in a blandly palpable way, and a secular house may bless the book.

I've heard anecdotally that book contracts to first-time authors make up only 20 percent of each sales cycle. Some book deals are given to people who are not writers by trade, but those with a recognized name and a message to tell that they put in the form of writing—"here is my revelation or post-tragic reflection, here is an insider's look into a vice or addiction, here is a memoir of my career." Writing is the medium, not the craft.

Meanwhile, there are many fine writers who are told "keep going" by agents but can't nab a book deal with a small online reach or a tiny number of newsletter subscribers. I'm a member of a few online groups filled with emerging writers. Every month or two in these spaces, I read a post that looks something like this:

> "I feel called to write a book, but I don't have a large enough platform, so I can't get a contract. What should I do?"

Comments are filled with people who can relate, and I am one of them. "Keep writing!" We tell them. "Try a lead magnet!

Beef up your mailing list!" "Have you considered a giveaway or guest blog post?"

Those of us that clear the hurdles by building up enough online engagement to publish a first book may be given a small advance. Advance money typically goes toward promoting the book, with a launch #squad on socials, giveaways, and maybe a book trailer. You will only make enough money to begin a career as a working author if your first book does well and you secure a multi-book deal, and it's a total grind.

Why do so many of us want to be published in the first place: what's at the heart of that impulse? What's the root of the tug? In a 2017 TED Talk, Anne Lamott sums up why writers write: "You're going to feel like hell if you wake up some day and you never wrote the stuff that is tugging on the sleeves of your heart. Your stories, memories, visions, and songs...in your own voice. That's really all you have to offer us, and that's also why you were born."

Lamott doesn't say we're born to publish books. In fact, she warns against publishing to fill a void. "Publication and temporary creative successes are something you have to recover from. They kill as many people as not. They will hurt, damage, and change you in ways you cannot imagine," she says. "It's also a miracle to get your work published...just try to bust yourself gently of the fantasy that publication will heal you. That it will fill the swiss-cheesy holes inside of you. It can't, it won't. But writing can."

As a Christian, I believe we need people to write about faith and culture, in spite of the emotional toll the publishing process may bring. More of us that are alert to the division and brokenness in the American church, and still writing about the pursuit of a deep relationship with God. We need more spaces to publish writing that explores this space, and a model that supports our voices.

I think of the line in Levertov's poem *The Springtime:* "They have a great space of dark to bark across." She's writing with desperation about change, life and death. But I began to wonder, what do you do when you're writing about Christianity from a different place, a middle place, and the dark you're barking across is exceptionally wide?

How I make decisions, interact in the world, and think through ethics and culture is plainly rooted in the teachings of Jesus. I know how that sounds, and what cultural currency it could cost me in some circles. But I also know that when you write honestly, cards face up, about where you're coming from, people tend to make space for you. I have a simple faith in a complicated world that my eyes are open to, and I hold both at the same time. But that also means there are few publications or publishers for people like me to land.

Essentially, I'm in the same place as any other writer, jumping through hoops, leveraging connections, and writing a book proposal to sell an idea to an editorial board. I am in no seat to judge while I jockey for a slot on a fall release list and try to save myself from the slush pile.

But instead of just showing up or competing, I'd like to champion other writers in this third space, writing about the tension of belief in Jesus in a culture when, against all odds, we really do.

Who are those of us in this scrappy cohort writing to, and how do we find each other? The traditional and Christian publishing models haven't been disrupted, and many new voices can't break through. We need a different way forward for Christians who are exploring topics that may be too insider for traditional media and too countercultural in faith-based spaces.

Here I am, and maybe you are, too. We're in the middle, looking for each other. The woods are wide and we're scattered on the path, but it leads to a clearing.

What if writing is never a career for most of us, but a practice that chooses us and encourages many? Those of us with eyes open, published and unknown, moving toward the storm. Telling better stories. We are here, we write because we are writers. God, do we ever believe. Help our unbelief.

Sara Billups
Writer & Co-host of Ebenezer Podcast

DOPAMINE AND A DEFENSE OF WRITING

L.T. Greer

I HATE TO WRITE.

It's time-consuming. It requires prolonged focus. It demands study, reflection, confrontation, written and rewritten sentences, rough drafts, and crumpled pages. And that's all before a piece is completed. After it's "finished," new torments emerge: the unanticipated argument, the missed typo, the now-obvious point, the intended audience's misapplication, the unintended audience's misunderstanding, that One Thing I would definitely add (or subtract) if I had the chance to do it again.

And if this wasn't enough, sitting down to write scores an entertainment value of close to nil. It cannot contend with the allure of the endless scroll. Writing tallies a *zero* for a quick-and-easy dopamine hit. And writing has virtually nothing to offer in the arenas of insta-fame or insta-rage. Indeed, the act of careful writing is so feeble in its power to lure, to entertain, to arouse, or to provoke that, in comparison to the competition's pervasive temptation and instant gratification, it's a wonder that I'm able at all to punctuate this very sentence. Wait. *...this very sentence!* That's better.

•••

I love to write.

Whatever superficial indulgences the alternatives have to offer, they can never plumb depths like the process of writing can. It's happening right now: study, reading, and personal experience all merging in this act of writing. To write is to seize an instrument for greater understanding. In writing, an intellectual alchemy begins to bubble and gurgle, and it's unlike anything my pocketable glowing rectangle can produce.

Writing guards against vague thinking. Complete sentences help to form complete thoughts. In casual conversation, I can refer to something that I thought I believed, only to find it derailed by a simple inquiry from my nine-year-old. Writing, however, forces a careful consideration of the reader, even if that reader will only be me. Clarity in writing is premised on clarity in thinking, and—curiously—the writing process helps to clarify thought. Writing forces the issue, exposes the holes, reveals the inconsistent, displays the contradictory. As the virtuous writing-thinking-writing circle spins up, errors are exposed, paths are illuminated, breakthroughs are made. The writer shapes the words, and the words shape the writer.

An implicit question for almost any seriously written word is simply, "Does this make sense?" Any sci-fi author on the receiving end of a tweet storm about the time-space continuum will tell you that even fantasy must be communicated sensibly. In this way, the act of writing provides an antidote to the toxic superficialities that other more passive forms of "engagement" propagate through their channels and feeds. Digital hyperbole can be shameless and self-contradictory precisely because it is bite-sized, mindless, ephemeral. They'll be all-caps YELLING something else in an hour. In contrast, a cohesively written piece has the powerful ally of carefully considered words—words that were first considered, then reconsidered, and finally wrestled down by their writer.

Writing clarifies, but clear thought is merely writing's penultimate gift. If clarified *thinking* is on the other side of clear writing, then clarified *belief* is on the other side of clear thought. Sound thinking helps to form and reform belief. "Be transformed by the renewal of your mind," said the apostle. My motivation for writing may be to clarify thinking, but my purpose for writing is to mold belief—beginning with myself and extending to others.

•••

We all believe something. My way of life, my ambitions, and my affections are premised on some supposition. What makes the good life? Which is the way to the desired destination? How is the preferred outcome achieved? All people are pursuing answers to these questions in one way or another. Even the most data-driven among us can't escape Pascal's wager. Each of us has laid our chips on the table. We all believe that something or other supplies the most promising pursuit of happiness.

Clarity of thought exposes existing beliefs and, critically, illuminates better ones. "The truth shall set you free," Jesus said. The liberating truth he referred to wasn't isolated in a diagnostic test tube or privatized in an individual boutique experience. "The truth," says Jesus in effect, "is that everyone is following something or someone; everyone practices discipleship to something." He is right. "If you abide in my word, you are truly my disciples. Then you will know the truth, and the truth shall set you free," he said. Here the Incarnate Word exhorts with his spoken word to abide in his written Word. He is calling anyone who would listen out of default, passive belief and into liberating, intentional belief.

This is why I write: to be set free from wonted belief, and to be drawn into accord with reality. My audience is me and people like me—in my church, in my neighborhood, and in my city. We are all confronted with a perpetual wall of noise that passively distracts and actively deceives. Without the exposure and relocation of our hearts' presuppositions, we are like those to whom Jesus was originally speaking—utterly beholden to and trapped by the very things we purport to authenticate our liberty. It is an especially devastating kind of entrapment to believe I am freed by that which entangles me.

But the inverse gives hope: the retuning of our hearts' beliefs to resonate with the truth. What if my job was no longer to survey and select from an ocean of self-actualization techniques? What if my task was no longer to synthesize "my truth" from the disparate parts of my own conflicting desires and an ever-changing zeitgeist? What if instead, someone made a way for me to sing in concert with a singular, radiant, created intent?

That would be freedom.

Now here we are—you and I, reader and writer—at the conclusion. Our conclusion has made bold claims, going so far as to invoke the grandiose themes of "truth" and "freedom." It's a conclusion that, at least for me, beckons. It is no easy path, yet it is far easier than sprinting to nowhere on the treadmill of the ordinary. It is a conclusion drawn only after the process and perspiration of writing.

L.T. Greer
Writer

POETRY PULLS THE SPLINTER OUT

On the Painful and Gratifying Process of Writing Poetry

Mike Bonikowsky

BEFORE THE POEM, THERE IS THE PAIN. Sometimes it's a good pain: a stab of delight, an ache of longing, a sudden blaze of joy. More often it is something else: the dull clanging alarms of anxiety, the hot tearing of rage, the long slow labour of the Maranatha agony.

The pain, whatever it is, grows until it can no longer be ignored, then continues to work its way deeper until it can no longer be borne. And then something must be done about it. Somehow or other, the splinter has to come out.

When I was young and knew no better, I would cut patterns on my skin and try to bleed it out. These days I'm more likely to yell at the kids or punch a hole in the drywall or lie under the covers scrolling down on my phone for hour after hour. But there is better, wiser, healthier catharsis, and its name is poetry.

•••

I first learned how to pull the splinters out in high school. There were so many of them in those days, as there are for all of us, and all the worse as I had not yet learned their names. I don't remember when or why, but one day I began writing down what hurt.

It started simply with individual words, scrawled down in a notebook with a plastic orange cover. I wasn't trying to write poems then, and would have been alarmed at the suggestion. It was an exorcism, an attempt at magic, naming the feelings in an attempt to get them out of me. To my immense surprise, I found that it worked. Writing it down is how the splinter comes out. It's the only way to determine its shape and its size, where it came from and what it means, if anything. The act of writing pulls the pain out, washes the blood off of it, and holds it up to the light where it can be seen for what it is.

I also thought it made me look cool, and might get girls to notice me. I was trying on identities, as we do at that age, and I liked the idea of being the guy in the corner, scribbling down... what? Who knew? It didn't matter. It didn't matter if it was good or not, because nobody would ever read it. But I was writing, which most people weren't, and that made me a writer, and it seemed like that or nothing. So I put on that identity like a mask, and I wear it still.

•••

High school ended, mercifully, and I enrolled in a small Christian university's social service worker program with the vague ambition of changing the world in some undefined way. By now the journal was an ever-present prop, now black and decorated with stickers designed to anger the more conservative of my classmates. I sat in dark corners wherever I could find them and scrawled away, hoping the corners were not too dark for girls to see what I was doing there.

And here grace enters the picture, for the mask began to change the face beneath it. You can't write regularly, even if the writing is part of a flimsy, self-serving persona, without getting better at it. I was scribbling away, mostly garbage, but I kept scribbling, and slowly things began to emerge that I had never imagined were there, better things than I had been trying for, truer things.

I begin to share some of the more coherent children of the journal with friends through the iconic pre-Facebook blog community Xanga. People liked what I wrote. They shared my words with other people. This threw gas on the fire, gave me a feeling I needed more and more of.

At the same time, I was beginning to feel more and more lost in my academic studies. Without a vocation, the social services seemed more and more incorporeal, the text books I read more and more a waste of money and time. But I was also taking the mandatory English literature course, which was setting my heart and mind on fire. The assignments and essays came easily to me, the reading a joy, and soon it was the only class I was passing. It soon became clear that I could become an English major, or drop out. I switched majors, and began to drown in an ocean of literature.

•••

Reading more, and better, caused me to write more, and better. I was now fully immersed in the persona of Poet, which had the sole benefit of forcing me to spend more time actually writing words on paper in order to maintain the illusion.

I won a few small contests within my school. I was published in the campus magazine, which immediately went to my head. I pushed it too far. Intoxicated by my tiny successes, I decided the time had come to burn my boats. I would quit my part-time job and devote myself fully to becoming a Real Writer, earning a living with my pen.

I failed, of course, so spectacularly that not only did I not produce any income with my writing, I didn't even produce any writing. I did produce some very respectful playthroughs of the Halo series, and a great deal of anxiety and self-hatred. I found myself with more splinters, not fewer, and now no way to remove them.

The truth is that I had never, and still do not, actually enjoy the act of writing. Sitting down to put the words on paper is a sensation akin to peeling the skin from my bones and walking around with every nerve exposed. It's not something one does recreationally. I don't write unless I absolutely have to. But the splinter gets in, and it works its way down into the center of me until I can't stand it anymore. Sooner or later the splinter comes between me and everything and everyone else, until it's all that I can see. This, and only this, is sufficient motivation for me to write. There are much easier ways to put food in my belly.

•••

I stopped pretending to be a writer and found a new job. The work I found was in the social services, a brutal and beautiful job caring for men and women with developmental disabilities. At the time I thought it would tide me over until I finished my degree and published a fabulously successful novel. This spring marks my fifteenth year in the field.

My work in the group home is the opposite of the position of Writer I aspired to hold. It is mostly physical and, dare I say, spiritual work. It does not engage the mind. It leaves very little time for introspection, and less for writing. It doesn't make you famous, and it does not get the girls to notice you. It is hidden work. It is the best thing that ever happened to me.

A strange thing happened when I gave up the literary life. As soon as I embraced what I now see was always my true vocation, and when leaned into it by acquiring a wife and several children to care for in what spare time remained, I finally became a writer. I no longer wrote to create an identity for myself. I had already been given more identity than I could bear.

I now write because I have to. My true life, the life of early mornings bathing wounded bodies and late nights comforting crying infants, has finally given me what I never had before— something to write about. Poems now squeeze out of the corners of my responsibility-packed days like oil from the joints of a machine. I am full of splinters all the time because my life is shared with other human beings, and we are always colliding.

The splinters must come out, and poetry is how. And they are, if not good poems, then at least true poems, poems born not of posture but of vocation. I have learned how to share them wherever I can, first on the internet with friends, then to journals such as this one, edited by generous and like-minded people.

This is the last step: polishing the splinter and showing it to whoever is passing by, to see if they know where it came from— what the splinter is made of. Sometimes, often even, I find that others are able to recognize the location and material of what used to just be poking me from the inside out.

Sometimes seeing the splinters in the light of day gives them the tools they need to remove it from their own hearts. And sometimes they, too, are able to see the face reflected in it, and we whisper His name to one another, and are comforted. He is in every created thing, even when those things have been shattered.

•••

The poems continued to come, always in their own time, never forced (except for the bad ones), each one a gift to me. They continued to be published by kind people. One of those kind people asked me to come on board this very journal as poetry editor, a post I held for a year. And out of that came an invitation to submit a chapbook to Solum Literary Press, and out of that comes my first published collection, *Red Stuff*. A gift, as it all has been.

It is always a relief to finish a poem. It feels as if I have emerged from deep water, gasping for air, and I always feel as if I will never write another one. But I always do. The world is blowing itself to hell, and there is always a splinter of something or other, working its way inward toward the heart.

We are all full of the shards and shrapnel of our own bombardments, both large and small. We are all the walking wounded. And though the world is full of sharp things shaped to injure, so has it been made full of balms and medicines and methods of healing. One of the ways we are made whole again is by putting our wounds into words. A poem pulls a splinter out, whether we know why we are scribbling or not.

Mike Bonikowsky
Writer & Developmental Service Professional

A LITERARY COMMUNITY, A KINGDOM

John Hawbaker & John B. Graeber

IT IS NOT GOOD FOR A WRITER TO BE ALONE.

It's necessary—for a time—or else the work won't get done. We can both attest to that. But once the paragraphs have been arranged, the sentences refined and word choices agonized over, most writing is meant to be shared.

Then what? Clicking "submit" or "publish" or "send tweet" doesn't form a meaningful connection. It simply makes the opportunity for connection possible. And social media can sometimes make a writer feel more connected than they really are.

What writers long for is to be known. As writers who tend to focus on chronicling and interpreting our experiences, we want our work to find a home in someone else's heart.

The rapid movement of social media makes this challenging. Any individual piece of writing can spread farther and faster than ever. But even with the best of intentions, the information flows relentlessly, and many readers move on to the next thing before getting three minutes into the article they've already clicked.

On the other hand, a writer may get a word of appreciation, or see a new insight into their work referenced in a tweet, but deeper conversation remains elusive.

When we attended the Festival of Faith and Writing in April, we saw the talent and generosity of writers burning brightly—and their lamps help light our own.

The festival sparked an affinity for discussing essays and poetry that we love with other writers. Seeing where those threads of conversation might go. Recognizing in our own work how something we've read has helped sculpt our own thoughts. Asking other writers how their writing evolves as they interact with the ideas and style of writers they admire and respect.

Both of us returned with fresh inspiration—to write more, to tackle new genres and to somehow pass on what we felt. Generosity and exploration emerged as motivating forces in our discussions. We wanted to celebrate works that meant something to us and help other people make new discoveries of their own. And we wanted to learn from writers whose work had taken up residence in our souls.

And so we started *Tributaries,* our monthly email newsletter, to celebrate great writing and to build community around it.

Social media, and Twitter in particular, introduces us to many of the pieces we feature. We then invite ourselves and our readers beyond the constant churn to really consider a timeless, high-quality work with the attention it deserves.

Our decision to release each issue early on Sunday mornings reflects this. The timing may seem counterintuitive, but we chose it in hopes that readers will take some extra time they may not have during the week to consider the contributions of our guest slowly and thoughtfully.

In our third issue, our guest Alia Joy wrote, "That's where creation happens, in the universality of human experience, thought, and emotion." That thought really captures what this project has come to mean. Even when the details of particular events diverge, there is a connection between us that exists on a deeper level and, paradoxically perhaps, it's in the specifics of our individual stories where we find the strongest connection. That's when we recognize the *Imago Dei* in each other.

Not many of us are bird-watchers like the subject of "Lord God Bird," which was Ashley Abramson's featured selection. But we all know what it feels like to experience the divine come to earth. To see something so far beyond our ability to comprehend that we're left simply to utter, "Lord God, look at that." We all know what that feels like, even if it comes to each of us differently.

Our desire to celebrate and discuss great writing in a public setting has a long and beautiful history that neither one of us were much attuned to.

The act of writers responding to their peers' published work in print or online has always existed, both for good and for ill. Joan Didion, Susan Sontag, Norman Mailer, Lionel Trilling, and others fired salvos back and forth in the pages of *The Partisan Review, The New York Review of Books,* and others in the mid-1900s.

Taking aim at a possibly more uplifting target than these 20th century literary figures, *Tributaries* joins that tradition, with a conscious decision to focus specifically on what's good and beautiful in the work of our contemporaries. It's intriguing, but ultimately not surprising, to find ourselves floating downstream in this wide river of public criticism that sprung out of the ground far behind us.

In her essay "Why I Write," Didion described writing as "imposing oneself upon other people, of saying listen to me, see it my way, change your mind."

Publication is an audacious act. As writers, we are saying to others, "Listen to my experience. Hear my ideas. They are worthy of your time." We believe they have value sufficient to compel others to read and consider them, to be molded by them and respond to them. That's what we're asking our *Tributaries* guests to do.

We dialogue not only with the thoughts of other writers, but their style as well. We consider ourselves poetry lovers, but also novices—"amateurs," or "lovers of" in the French. So it was a blessing to invite Carolina Hinojosa-Cisneros as a guest and have her help us better understand what made her selection, "The Slaughter" by Quina Aragon, so moving.

Quina hadn't experienced such an in-depth analysis of her writing, and she shared that Carolina's observations helped her better grasp her own work. "It affirmed the gifts and burdens I believe God has given me, and it has pushed me to want to grow even more in my craft," she said. "It felt so affirming to see that writers I admire actually admire my writing as well."

Brian Doyle's essay "Joyas Voladoras," chosen by Nick Ripatrazone for our first issue, is a remarkable piece of writing to explore stylistically. Doyle manages to weave commentary on hummingbirds together with profound insight into the nature of the human heart, and the impact is shattering. Ripatrazone helped us, and our readers, dig into how Doyle accomplished the feat.

From a scriptural perspective, the most direct inspiration for *Tributaries*—although it wasn't consciously part of our thinking as we developed the concept—is Philippians 4:8. Eugene Peterson's idiomatic translation has a poetic ring to it:

> *Summing it all up, friends, I'd say you'll do best by filling your minds and meditating on things true, noble, reputable, authentic, compelling, gracious—the best, not*

the worst; the beautiful, not the ugly; things to praise, not things to curse.

In addition to "the beautiful" and "things to praise" found in the structure or style of a work, *The Message* includes another word that resonates when you consider many of the pieces we've discussed over the past six months: "authentic."

While sometimes overused, especially in a certain Christian cultural context, the inclusion of "authentic" in this verse is striking. It points beyond "true," which is often code for doctrine or presuppositions, to the human experience.

We've discussed numerous written works that delve deeply into anxiety, depression, injustice, and grief. Without fail, these unflinching portrayals of the authors' experiences read more like Psalms than church service testimonies. We've found in our conversations with other writers, as well as with *Tributaries* readers, that these pieces have opened up space to think and feel differently about their own difficult experiences.

These works, and our conversations, seem to be living up to our goal of helping people feel less alone in the world, thanks to their authenticity.

While we don't exclusively interview writers who are Christian, or only discuss works by Christian writers, the community we're creating is marked by Christian character. We focus on what's authentic, true, and written with excellence and beauty. We don't ignore pain but we shift our eyes—and hearts—away from the bickering and strife that tends to dominate the news cycles and social media.

The world abounds in anger. Much of it is righteous, because there's a lot of brokenness in the world and we're not healing it quickly enough. But sometimes the outrage harms rather than helps.

From the beginning, we have wanted *Tributaries* to put the true, pure, and authentic into the world. We want to celebrate what's good, and to stir up empathy and hope.

It's only fitting to end our meditation on this project with the words of a guest, Ashley Abramson:

> Discussing works of other writers adds a sense of urgency and vitality to the larger conversation of Christian art, and art in general, reminding us this work isn't just for ourselves, but for the coming of the Kingdom, for the sanctification of the saints. Discussing other writers' work points us back to the larger story, the narrative we're all chipping away at with our words and stories.

John Hawbaker & John B. Graeber
Founders of *Tributaries*

CRITICISM

EDUCATION FOR AN ETERNAL KINGDOM

Doug Sikkema

Aeneas sank his blade in fury in Turnus' chest.
Then all the body slackened in death's chill,
And with a groan for that indignity
His spirit fled into the gloom below.

Vergil. *Aeneid* XII. 1295–1298

"IT'S CALLED A WHISKER," the esteemed sociologist told me, pointing at a series of PowerPoint slides with dots spattered across the Cartesian plane like a piece of bad modern art. The dots had horizontal lines shot through them. These were whiskers.

It was a beautiful day, several years ago now, and the quieted Notre Dame campus was in the full flush of God's yearly exhalation. The dead embers of the recently-dormant campus ground were now being whispered into a stunning blaze of colors. And here I was, a senior researcher for a think tank, stuck in a windowless board room staring at dots and whiskers on screens upon screens.

"The whisker is significant," he went on, "because it tells us the variations of responses for each variable. Therein lies the story!" He was excited. Too excited I thought. To the untrained eye—to my eye, at the time—these slides were like ancient hieroglyphics: amusing to look at, but meaningless. There was no story I could discern. What was unique about the data was that we were not just interested in what kind of jobs graduates had, or how much money they made. Rather, we wanted to know their habits and dispositions, their marital and family status, and how much they gave to charity and served the community.

Driving this research project was a simple question: Did the school sector you attended in your youth shape the kind of man or woman you became? I won't get into the more wonky and technical side of the data procurement that allowed "school sector" to be isolated from other variables (like socioeconomic status, ethnicity, gender, etc.). But that summer, after the initial migraine had subsided from taking a crash course in statistics and data analysis, the story in the slides slowly started to emerge. And part of the story was that graduates in Canadian Christian schools were not likely to be in positions of cultural influence. They were, broadly speaking, less likely than graduates of other sectors to be politicians, cultural influencers, or even wealthy CEOs of companies. As we sat around with academics, pollsters, sociologists, and statisticians, the question was how we would frame this narrative in the report. Why did it seem that graduates from this sector were not excelling? Why were they not excellent? Why were they not, by all the metrics our survey was meant to track, great?

•••

Excellence. The Greek's called it *arete,* a word which later Christians would translate as virtue. Their literature is filled with characters who embody it. When the Greeks were overtaken by

Rome, their cultural influence endured and, in many ways, the notion of excellence, or virtue, persisted in Roman literature, which was a main source of educational formation. There was no sociological data, thank heavens, to track how effective this was, but part of a training in excellence required inculcation into a literary and cultural tradition that held excellence on display. Story revealed a greatness worthy of imitation.

During Rome's imperial phase, a young Roman's education would inevitably lead to an encounter with Aeneas, survivor of decimated Troy and founder of Roma, the eternal city. The young Roman would learn of the Trojan war by way of the Greek Homeric epics, to be sure, but in addition to *The Iliad* and *The Odyssey,* young boys and girls would learn the tales of Aeneas by memorizing vast swaths of Vergil's Latin epic, *The Aeneid.*

Commissioned by Caesar Augustus—yes, the same Augustus whose decree of a census would send a lowly carpenter and his pregnant wife off to some nondescript town in the farthest reaches of the empire—the story of Aeneas was meant to be instructive and formative for young Romans. For a well-heeled Roman, not only was Vergil's account a primer of the most exquisite use of Latin, but it provided an education in theology, philosophy, and history, while also attending to the more practical matters of hospitality and statecraft. The epic provided Romans with a mythology fit for an empire seeking not only dominance, but a new era of peace, a Pax Romana that might put an end to endless war. The epic did not simply tell a story for entertainment but revealed a form of life worthy of admiration and praise, and worthy of imitation. Aeneas, then, was an exemplar of the distinctly Roman ideal for the good life: courageous, eloquent, wise, crafty, industrious, and disciplined.

But above all, Vergil reiterates that Aeneas is pious. Piety for the Romans was not the priggish self-righteousness that the word might connote today. Rather, in Vergil's sense, pietas was to be duty-bound to something greater than the self, such as the will of the gods or the good of the State. This is Roman excellence.

For this reason, Aeneas spurns (okay: eventually spurns) the sexual wiles of the Carthaginian Queen Dido and the tempting lure to rule alongside her. No matter how much Aeneas might want these things, they are not the role the gods have prescribed for him. He must sacrifice his security and even his bodily pleasures and submit to his God-given task of seeing the new Troy founded. There's a lot to Aeneas's Roman piety that a Christian might rightly admire.

But Roman pietas was also justification for merciless cruelty. In the final scene of the epic, Aeneas and Turnus, the prince of the Rutulians, engage in hand-to-hand combat for the fate of the Latin people. Aeneas eventually gains the upper hand and holds his enemy's life in his hands. Turnus bravely accepts his fate, but not without making one final appeal to Aeneas for mercy to spare his life. Aeneas considers briefly but opts for vengeance and plunges his sword deep into the heart of his enemy. The earth is awash in blood. Troy—that enduring symbol of human ingenuity, power, and strife—rises anew in the form of Rome.

The epic ends here, abruptly. How it might have concluded if Vergil had lived a while longer is scholarly speculation. Regardless, the epic, in its current form profoundly shaped the moral imagination of the burgeoning Empire that would rule the Western world with bureaucratic sophistication, awe-inspiring opulence, and an ironclad fist for centuries to come.

•••

"Dad, was Aeneas a good man?" My daughter asked this at dinner the other night. She is in third grade. In their school, they are studying Ancient history and being introduced to some of the earliest stories in cultural memory. They are learning about Genesis and the Old Testament alongside children's versions of the *Epic of Gilgamesh, The Iliad* and *The Odyssey, The Code of Hammurabi,* and, yes, *The Aeneid.* Like the early Greeks and Romans, we too want our children's imaginations furnished with characters worthy of admiration and imitation.

Our daughter and her brothers attend Oak Hill Academy, a classical Christian school my wife and I helped start here in our hometown of Hamilton, Ontario. There are a few reasons that we and our small-but-growing community are intrigued by the classical Christian model, not least of which is our desire to nurture eight-year-olds capable of even asking such questions. Because one aspect of the classical model of education we love is its desire to intentionally introduce our children to some of the greatest literature and thought in the human tradition.

Now I consider myself fairly well educated. I have a Bachelor of Arts degree and a Bachelor of Education, and two graduate degrees: a Master's and a Doctorate. However, for none of these degrees was I required to read or even be remotely familiar with *The Iliad* or *The Odyssey;* Plato or Socrates or Epicurus; Homer or Hesiod; Aeschylus or Sophocles; Herodotus, Livy, or Eusebius; Vergil or Cicero; not to mention, Jerome, Augustine, Boethius, Aquinas, Dante. The list goes on.

My understanding of this philosophical, religious, aesthetic, and literary tradition was self-taught outside the curriculum expectations of the primary, secondary, and multiple post-secondary schools I attended. There are still many gaps. I am now an assistant professor at Redeemer University where I teach portions from such texts in a core program designed, in part, to introduce students (many for the first time) to the riches that precede them. Unfortunately for most of my students, and even many of my colleagues, such omissions in Canadian education—private, Christian, or otherwise—have been the rule, not the exception. One student at the end of our semester frustratedly asked the question—a question that should burn for anyone who has discovered late in life what's been withheld from them—"Why did no one tell us about this inheritance?"

I like this idea of an inheritance, and even the delightful presumption that it's ours. Indeed, something of value is being gifted to us in such works. Of course, this is not to say the inheritance is beyond question or critique. There are ideas and assumptions that might—and often should—offend and scandalize us. (Whether or not Aeneas is a "good man" still needs an answer, I know!) But the pervasive hermeneutic of suspicion, employed in many institutions of higher learning, has helped to castigate such texts from the curriculum wholesale. On top of this, a utilitarian vision for education and economic crises have often gutted the curriculum of such content in favor of employable hard and soft skills.

But if and when you journey with Dante to the Beatific vision at the end of *Paradiso* or you hear the comforting music of Lady Philosophy to Boethius as he awaits his untimely death; and if you cringe to hear the wicked wisdom Nicolo Machiavelli bestows on a young Prince or get lost in the deliciously rebellious rhetoric of Milton's Satan; you must ask yourself: what sort of culture would hold back such riches—even with their flaws—from the next generation? And what might be the consequences of this great withholding?

•••

Education is the transmission of culture from one generation to the next. It really is that simple. And when we eliminate such texts from the culture we pass on, we are all the poorer for it. But more, the child who becomes the adult with little to no sense of the past is uprooted from time, captivated by a pervasive presentism that lends itself to both ennui and shock, malaise and hysteria. Cultivating a healthy knowledge and, dare I say, a reverence of what has come before us, roots us in healthy ways to our place and time, our here and now. With the right education, this inheritance truly can be, and should be, ours. But was Aeneas a good man?

"The good man speaking well." At the Regents School of Austin, you'll find these words carved in the beautiful yellow-brown limestone of their Rhetoric building. Regents is a classical Christian school and this phrase, deceptively simple as it seems, is perhaps the best summation of what classical Christian education is after and why it's so urgently needed today. The telos of classical education is the cultivation of good, virtuous, wise people.

The engraved phrase comes from Quintilian's *Institutio Oratoria*, a thorough compendium of oratorical theory building on Greek thought from Isocrates and Roman predecessors like Cato and, of course, Cicero. For Quintilian, oratory should not be detached from virtue or character. An eloquent person who lacked virtue was monstrous, a clever devil. Or, as the apostle Paul phrased it to his Corinthian audience: "You might speak with the tongues of men and of angels, but if you have not love, you are just a resounding gong." But did the Romans really know what it meant to be good?

•••

When Christianity overtook paganism as the dominant religion of the Roman empire, it might not surprise us that the education of Antiquity became problematic for the early Church. Some Christians even advocated that the writings of folks like Vergil and Quintilian should be discarded in favor of the gospels and Pauline epistles and early Church Fathers. But Augustine, a North African Bishop from the 4th century, advocated a more nuanced and charitable approach to the very good accomplishments of the God-denying pagans he, at least, cherished from his education.

These works, he believed, prepared his heart for the good news of Christ. For Augustine, the inarguable goods of the pagan classical world, then, should be considered like the Egyptian gold the Israelites used to adorn their temple. While the Egyptians wrongfully used it in false worship, the gold was gold, nonetheless. It might be still be used in service to the living God. The trick was learning how to look and see, listen and hear what is true, good, and beautiful and knowing that any such things come only from God, their source.

Remarkably, Augustine advocated for this charitable approach to the founding literature of Rome as the idea of Rome was starting to crumble, and the ever-precarious Pax Romana was coming to a violent end. With the sacking of Rome, Augustine knew firsthand how temporal the eternal city really was. To Augustine, Rome was not what Vergil or Augustus or any of the Romans educated in that particular tradition imagined it to be. Despite all its goodness, Rome—and Aeneas its founder—embodied the *libido dominandi*, the lust for domination. For Augustine and the early Christian church, Rome epitomized the City of Man that waged eternal war against the City of Heaven. It was a Roman cross that held a dying Christ. It was Romans, Matthew's gospel records, who laughed and mocked, tortured and killed the Son of God. The final thrust of Aeneas's sword is the endgame of Roman pietas. The dying breath of Christ is the endgame of Christian pietas.

•••

As the leaves turned and the data report on graduate outcomes neared completion, it became increasingly apparent that our late-modern world had shared assumptions about what made a graduate great. And even a Christian think tank was not immune from imbibing some of these default cultural assumptions. There was a tacit picture of what success looked like: marriage, family, piety, to be sure, but we also wanted (even if we were afraid to say it), status, influence, power, celebrity. We live in the Pax Americana, the long, dubious, precarious peace of the postwar world. And in this world the aspirations we have—or have for our children—are shaped and misshaped by the culture and its false gods. When we long for greatness, even with the best of intentions, do we know what we are longing for?

The twentieth century witnessed the *libido dominandi* potently in the Third Reich. Nazi Germany was really only one more manifestation of the new Rome and Adolf Hitler—talk about eloquent devils—the strong arm of a new Aeneas sent to usher in the imperial might of a new empire for a new Germany. But nothing is new. In the chaos of the second world war and displaced by German occupation, the French mystic and philosopher Simone Weil reflected on what the rise of Nazi Germany and the collapse of the French meant. In *The Need for Roots*, Weil argued in 1943—with no clear end or victory in sight—that the terror of the Germans and the easy destruction of the French were related phenomena. Both sides, she argued, lacked the proper moorings of a moral education. Both French and German youth had grown indifferent to, and even unashamedly supportive of, power-hungry demagogues.

How, she wondered in 1943 before the war's end, could the West survive if an entire population—Christian and otherwise—truly believed Hitler, in all his vicious might was not just a good man, but a great man who could, in turn, make a nation great? Weil argued there was only one solution, and it had to do with education: "The only punishment capable of punishing Hitler, and deterring little boys thirsting for greatness in coming centuries from following his example, is such a total transformation of the meaning attached to greatness that he should thereby be excluded from it."

Weil wanted an education that would help her generation survive the war. Today, we still need this education to help us survive our peace. And a classical Christian education must never lose the accent on its second modifier. As a Christian education it is not merely about introducing our children to the human tradition, but guiding them through it by the illuminating truth of God's revealed Word. Such an education aspires to cultivating a good person by offering a vision of goodness—of greatness—that turns the hellbent logic of the City of Man on its head.

When Christ came to usher in His Kingdom, he entered a world dominated by Rome. Like Augustus, Christ too desired an eternal kingdom and a lasting peace. But He ushered it in as a weak child, a friend of outcasts, living in a remote corner of the world. After ministering for several years, He gave himself up to be betrayed by His people and, finally, was crushed under the yoke of Rome's pious might.

Was Aeneas a good man? Do we see ourselves in him? While there is much that is admirable in Aeneas, he must be turned inside out first. We, as natural born children of the City of Man, must also be turned around, converted, transformed. We must be set on another way. And that is what Christ came to do, to turn Roma inside out and show the way of *amor,* of love. If our children, through their education, can encounter such greatness, desire it, praise, admire, imitate it: then they are ready to live in the City of Man as citizens of the City of God.

Doug Sikkema
Writer & Professor

A TENDERNESS TOWARD ART

Michael Wright

> I have fallen in love with a painting... I have felt the energy and life of the painting's will; I have been held there, instructed. And the overall effect, the result of looking and looking into its brimming surface as long as I could look, is love, by which I mean a tenderness toward experience, of being held with an intimacy with the things of the world.
>
> **Mark Doty**

YOU DON'T HAVE TO FALL IN LOVE with a painting. It's okay to stand in front of an abstract painting in a museum and feel nothing. Or to walk briskly through a gallery, wondering if the attendant is guessing your income by your clothes. It's okay to be frustrated, even intimidated, by capital A-Art. I feel all of these things myself from time to time, even after years of exploring the contemporary art scene in Los Angeles. The truth is this: art is not a single thing, but a language of speaking through materials and colours and shape as old as Adam and Eve and as common as air. But like any language, learning to speak and understand it takes time and the steady insistence to push past our own confusion or insecurities to really appreciate it. I hope you can receive this encouragement from fellow Christian and art-lover Sister Wendy Beckett of what can happen if we look slowly, if we keep trying to learn this visual language for ourselves: "If we wait, each of us will find a way to experience that challenge that great art alone can offer. It is in the waiting, the seeking, the refusal to pretend that matter" (*Joy Lasts: On the Spiritual in Art*).

And do you know Sister Wendy's favourite painters, by the way? It's not Michelangelo painting his Sistine Chapel or an anonymous iconographer—it's Paul Cézanne. Cézanne, whose paintings have no discernible religious subject matter but instead use fractured textures to paint the ordinary world. So what gives? Why does this nun feel just as connected to these still life paintings as a cathedral fresco? Or better yet, why is it so easy for us to enjoy figurative paintings of the gospels but so difficult to engage contemporary art today—especially the weird, abstract, and confusing stuff—with the same level of patience and appreciation? What would we see if we pushed through our insecurities and looked beyond the art and artists that we're comfortable with?

I don't know what you'd see where you live, but I can tell you what I see in Los Angeles. After years of exploring the galleries and museums, there are so many artists who are creating work with explicit spiritual longings that I'm starting to lose track. There are group shows about pagan rituals, performance pieces that copy church services to riff on the financial and emotional struggles of artists, rituals that seek to access spiritual dimensions in gallery spaces, and literally redemptive sculptures made out of building debris from the Watts riots.

Not a single one of these things references Jesus or the psalms or Christian theology. Not one is stained glass inside a church building. Yet, all of this work—and the artists who make them—have become for me a cloud of witnesses that help me understand my own faith, that have given me a visual language for my spiritual journey. They could all be our conversation partners, these spiritually inflected artists. Do we have eyes to see?

Certainly in the gospels, Jesus embodies this question as he talks with people who are marginalized by the religious communities and institutions of the day. Tax agents and bleeding women, demonized Roman guards and the mentally distressed—Christ walks right past the social boundaries that exclude and marginalize and sits down for a meal. I couldn't help but think of scenes like this when I was a guest at an artist's recent house party, seated at the same table with MFA grads, queer art historians, and atheists—I start to tear up even writing about it. Yes they were chatting about their next shows, but they were also talking about financial survival, about how to pay rent at a studio and an apartment while still keeping their passion for their work alive. If you listened below the words, you could hear the questions they were asking: Is my art good? How do I become more honest with my own creative self? Will people enjoy this art as much as I do? How long will I be able to afford to do this? These were the unspoken longings at that table, and it was a holy gift to be there to listen, a guest in a world so often misunderstood by our own communities.

I'm sharing this not to critique, but to prod, to turn my own curiosity and passion for the arts back to the religious communities that formed me. In my own experience at a faith and arts organization (as both a student and employee), I was baffled at our lack of relationship-building with two museums within walking distance of our own offices. At times, it can even feel that the faith and art conversation is so insular that we're only talking to ourselves and forgetting our own neighbours. So are we aware of recent activism at museums or social practice art or exhibitions exploring art and mysticism? When contemporary art hosts conversations about spirituality, where are Christian voices? When artists struggle with rising studio rents, where are my fellow Christians who would feed these artists if only they knew the address? Who would love this art if only we were active and patient in our looking?

I have to believe what's happening is not malicious, but the result of an unintentionally limiting vision. Here's what I mean: A few years ago, I went to a conference to hear a prominent faith and art leader speak. She was the keynote lecturer, and halfway through her speech she came to her fundamental thesis: "all art is doxological." In other words, for Christians engaged in the arts, the fundamental meaning of art is worship—art is meaningful insofar as it can conform to the conceptual grids of theology and worship. My heart sank. Of course, some art is this way: icons and hymns, stained glass, a psalm, medieval paintings. But what about the spiritually inflected still life paintings or those abstract sculptures made from debris? Works like this and the artists who make them have a spiritual resonance that doesn't fit within the liturgical shape of Sunday morning worship.

So let me be frank: starting with worship and liturgy as interpretive frames for the arts limits what could be a holistic and deeply compassionate engagement with art in its widest sense, this shared human language extending beyond Sunday morning. And if we can't cultivate this larger view, we'll miss an opportunity to participate in a larger conversation and to support the artists themselves. With even a quick skim of a book like *Creative Spirituality: The Way of the Artist,* you'll see story after story of artists leaving the church to make their art. This isn't just an aesthetic issue; we have a pastoral crisis. So what can be done?

First of all: nothing. I worry that any new Christian Vision for the Arts™ could quickly lead to misunderstanding what needs to be grassroots and focused on local art communities. No, I don't think we have to do anything other than crack open the door, walk into a local museum or gallery or artist studio and start asking new questions. Questions like: What would happen if churches provided low-cost studio space to local artists? What would a conference look like if it was built in collaboration with your city's art museum? What would it look like to offer chaplaincy for artists? How could churches use centuries of spiritual traditions to help curators inspire their museum-goers? Questions like these are too large to ask alone, so let's look around us and find artists and art lovers to answer them together. Who knows what will unfold!

And if any of this sounds daunting, we can always try small steps like these: check out an episode of "Art Assignment" (YouTube) or "Art21" (PBS), download the Artsy app and scroll around to see what artists are making, visit a gallery, listen to the "Modern Art Notes" podcast and subscribe to the "Hyperallergic" newsletter, visit a student show at the local art school, read books like *Art and Fear* and *Seven Days in the Art World*. These are all small steps we can take to get acquainted with the larger art world, and I promise you'll find something unexpected to inspire you and your church community.

What I'm aiming for is the vision the poet Mark Doty described in *Still Life with Oysters and Lemon: On Objects and Intimacy:* an "intimacy with the things of the world," an intimacy with the arts that is fundamentally incarnational, the very intimacy Christ himself experienced with the world. After a quick glance at our Twitter timelines, Lord knows we need this. And if I've learned anything from growing up in the church and working at a seminary, it's that the church—the people, at our best, embodying Christ—would be the perfect community to help sustain and celebrate the kind of humanizing and vital art we all need today.

Michael Wright

Writer, Editor & Educator

THE END OF DESIRE

Abbey Sitterley

MY NAME WAS ALMOST BRONWYN. When it came to deciding what to call her firstborn, my mother, an avid reader of fantasy novels from a young age, thought the quasi-mortal with arcane powers in Katherine Kurtz's *Deryni* novels would be a fine namesake. Grandma struggled pronouncing it, however, so my parents went with Abigail instead. Though the dream name wasn't bestowed, the favorite genres of the mother were visited upon the daughter. Turns out, fantasy novels are my not-so-guilty pleasure.

Mom kept my younger years well-stocked with her copies of Anne McCaffrey's *Dragonriders of Pern* series, Lewis's *Space Trilogy*, Tolkien's *The Lord of the Rings*, Ursula K. LeGuin's *A Wizard of Earthsea*, and Marion Zimmer Bradley's Arthurian epic *The Mists of Avalon* (the latter reserved for my teens). These books, with their rich imagery and lore, were more than just the means of escapism that fantasy's reputation is often demoted to. Each one wrestled with its own existential questions, moral dilemmas, and complicated relationships. Don't get me wrong, not all dragons were didactic, but their narratives shaped more than just my appreciation for a good tale. Stories teach as much as they entertain.

•••

When I became a Christian in 2014, the light of faith overtook everything in my life—especially my reading list. Alongside my search for books on theology, church history, and even religious rebuttals, I wanted good Christian fiction. Specifically, good Christian fantasy. I first turned to Lewis's *Space Trilogy* for the second time, this time with new eyes. In my search for more like it, I found much of the Christian fantasy selection wanting. Most of the books I sifted through tended to compromise on either the gravity of Christianity or an original plot. Stephen R. Lawhead's *Pendragon Cycle* provided some welcome respite in my quest, but I wanted more. So I kept looking. Thanks in part to my familiarity with C.S. Lewis and ilk, it wasn't long until I found the guy I call "the wizard of Christian fantasy"—Charles Williams.

Imagine this: stories that combine all the sorcerous mystery of Marvel's *Dr. Strange* with the religious-lore adventurism of *Indiana Jones,* while staying rooted in the allegorical depth of Lewis's *Narnia.* If that thematic blend piques your interest, you might like Charles Williams. Often referred to as "the forgotten Inkling," Williams was one of the more integral members of Oxford University's informal literati faculty group of the 1930s and 1940s: The Inklings. On staff with the Oxford University Press in various roles until his death, Williams enjoyed a prolific writing career.

Sadly, Williams's notoriety in Christian spheres of influence is pale in comparison to his fellow Inklings J.R.R. Tolkien and C.S. Lewis. Though all three wrote fantastical religious allegories, Williams's work has gotten lost in the shuffle. But to pass by Williams is to miss out on the kind of Christian art we need more of today. In a religious fiction market that is oversaturated with bludgeoning evangelistic messages and predictable storylines, Williams is a weird and much-needed bucket of cold water.

From poetry collections steeped in Arthurian legend, to literary criticism of Dante and Milton, a series of plays, and Christian fantasy novels, much of his work revolved around a concept he called "romantic theology." This, alongside an early penchant for mystical religious orders, operate as the two main pillars of Williams's magical world-building. To more deeply appreciate his work, it's best to know these engines.

•••

Romantic theology, according to Williams, should not be confused with the kind of flippant emotionalism the term conjures in us. "This term does not imply, as will inevitably at first be thought, a theology based merely on fantasy and dream, and concerning itself only with illogical sentimentalities." Quite the contrary, Williams's concept is too earthly to be solely ephemeral, and too self-sacrificial to be indulgently fleshy. He writes, "It is a theology as exact as any other kind, but having for cause and subject those experiences of man which, anyhow in discussions of art, are generally termed 'Romantic.' The chief of these is romantic love; that is, sexual love between a man and a woman, freely given, freely accepted, and appearing to its partakers one of the most important experiences in life—a love which demands the attention of the intellect and spirit for its understanding and its service."

Though one with seemingly lofty ideas, Charles Williams was no hypocrite. Borrowing from his years as a member of Christian mystic group The Fellowship of the Rosy Cross, Williams applied the tenets of romantic theology and founded The Companions of the Co-Inherence. According to his biographer, Alice Mary Hadfield, "co-inherence" was Williams's primary tenet of romantic theology. Co-inherence, to Williams, meant that if we are one in Christ, we must "bear each other's burdens" through "substitution" and "exchange." Though the heart of romantic theology is eros, the corporate form explored here is a devoted, Christ-quickened *philos,* where the chief virtue is to "lay down one's life for one's friends."

This principle of co-inherence is present in one form or another in each of Williams's novels, and acts as a sort of Rosetta Stone in unlocking a deeper layer within already entertaining narratives. Usually anchored in the discovery of some ancient religious artifact, such as the tesseract-like Stone of Solomon of Many Dimensions or the Holy Graal found in *War in Heaven,* each story demonstrates both the earthly function and eternal futility of human will, made its true self only in self-sacrifice.

•••

But while Williams's novels are certainly deeply layered with theological ruminations, he doesn't skimp on rich narrative, clever dialogue, and steady pace. *War in Heaven,* for example, transplants the legend of the Holy Graal to the English countryside and pits a depraved literary publisher and his fellow magicians against a jovial Archdeacon, a publishing agent, and a Duke as they all vie for the powerful cup of Christ. Unsurprisingly reminiscent of C.S. Lewis's *That Hideous Strength* (which Tolkien claimed was heavily influenced by Williams), Arthurian legend is sprinkled about the narrative as Williams bridges the past and present under the Graal quest and explores the *philos* expression of co-inherence.

A much more occult-driven tale, *The Greater Trumps* centers around a rumored deck of tarot cards that have the ability to control the weather. Again, a cast of characters attempt to control an artifact way beyond their ken, and are tossed into what Williams calls, "the Dance" at the center of all things. Since Williams was a one-time acolyte of A.E. Waite, co-creator of the well-known Rider-Waite deck and founder of the Rosy Cross, it's no surprise tarot makes an appearance.

Thus, perhaps what is best about Williams's storytelling is his courage to bridge the allure of magic with the uncompromising truth of Christianity under the banner of engaging narratives. In each story, characters on each side of the hero-villain divide attempt to enact their will upon an eternal thing and find themselves—not only despite but through their freedom of choice—bound to a Will much greater.

Gregory Persimmons, the literary magician hellbent on the Graal in *War in Heaven,* finds his plans consistently foiled by something higher than he, and yet continues to lash out in service of his lord, Satan. He soon comes to realize that all his strategy and machinations have done nothing but bring about a greater victory for good in the end. In a similar vein, the character Mornington later reflects on having assaulted Persimmons on account of his blasphemous language. The Archdeacon admonishes him for this behavior, as Mornington had acted out of the same spirit of hate Persimmons partakes in. "But he insulted God," Mornington insists. The Archdeacon replies, "How can you insult God? ...about as much as you can pull His nose." The best laid plans of mice and men are merely parlor games in the end.

•••

As our modern conception of romantic love tends to err strongly on the side of a narrow, self-indulgent form of eros, so does our modern Christian storytelling often default to bland regurgitations of secular "been-there-done-thats." This is what makes Charles Williams so refreshing. His narratives are not evangelistic attempts to make converts of his readers, nor do they eschew their allegorical and theological richness for the sake of more palpable themes.

Christian fiction of this stripe is the prescription we need for both our half-hearted evangelism and lackluster narratives. Much like the legacies of Lewis and Tolkien, Williams allows the interplay of narrative and theology to run wild through the fields of his imagination and the result is impactful and timeless, albeit lesser noted.

Here, Christian belief is portrayed as a reality to be taken seriously with story as its core, not merely its vehicle. It's this assertion that allows Williams to traverse the occult-religious divide with such grace. God isn't threatened by our silly attempts to control, because the playing field isn't even. How can you insult God? About as much as you can pull His nose. But as Williams's novels attest, wild things can happen when you try.

•••

When I was younger, I'd often take my favorite stories to a secret place. Sometimes the middle branches of an apple tree, sometimes a hollowed overgrowth of blackberry vines in the woods. There, my imagination bloomed alongside a growing need to keep special stories sacred; to be patient and savor them, set aside time for full attention, and be overtaken by what seemed just a breath beyond the veil between worlds.

As I grow closer to thirty, my ritual still stands. I'm taking my time with Williams nice and slow, still a few adventures left before my last. As I read *War in Heaven* this winter, curled up on a warm window seat in my kitchen, my mind drifted to the future recommendations I hope to make to my children. "Wait til you get a load of these," I'll tell them, unearthing a crate full of volumes as my mother did with me. Williams will maintain his place in the stacks, and I'll partake in the same zeal my mother felt, the cycle continuing. But that's the thing with fantasy: it's always "ever after." Even so, I think I'll take my time.

Abbey Sitterley
Writer & Musician

WIDENING THE OPENING

Eréndira Ramírez-Ortega

I'M AWARE OF THE CURIOSITY that is surfacing fervently about the creative work of people of color. We hear about how "our voices need to be heard," or "our stories need to be shared." To us, it seems we are living our ordinary lives, but being ordinary doesn't seem to be tragic enough.

It appears the ordinary among us have become a novelty because the moment someone who looks like us does something great, we are asked about it from the emotional (how does it feel?) to the intellectual (why do you think there aren't more people who look like you in the industry?).

Truth is, we need to postpone our walks to the park to toss a football with our children in order to answer all these things. Our opinions are elicited when something sinister is afoot, like when there is another explosive exposé into some event that happened in the industry, or when someone who looks like us is appointed into the echelons of the highest court of the land, despite our political inclinations, or when they receive an award in the literary or publishing machine and the gate-keepers—publishers, editors, agents, conference directors, writing department heads, Christian writers—are barely learning about it.

We're in a reckoning, it seems, literarily speaking.

We're asked to indulge now, and ruminate on our feelings about the reckoning—the coded "everything that is going on right now in the publishing world." Someone somewhere got harassed or got paid less or was misrepresented; and because we look like that person, the rest of us, by default, are expected to react.

•••

I recall the halls of the academe, how they towered with authority and imposition, insisting the believer conform to the philosophies of the spirit of the age, the kindling fire that beseeched me to "beware lest any man spoil you through philosophy and vain deceit, after the tradition of men, after the rudiments of the world, and not after Christ."

I earned my MFA in creative writing at Mills College, a female institution in the bay area. I was forewarned as I beheld mounted figureheads of the thought leaders that navigated me through treacherous waters, toward unknown destinations.

And yet, I awoke shipwrecked, so I designed makeshift fortresses to protect myself—and from what exactly?

Those of us who emerged from MFA programs confronted a mainstream literary culture that was unforgiving and relentless. While it was rewarding to have been published successively during and after the MFA, the price was brutal.

I didn't quite know then what course my life would take but I persevered. I was successful in the various academic institutions where I taught writing. Mills College served as a microcosm of what I eventually experienced in academia as an instructor and, ultimately, in the corporate world. The MFA also served as a microcosm of publishing, where prejudice and bias were pervasive.

I recall an office-hours meeting with a tenured faculty in the MFA, a woman of color, who stated that the application pool was lacking inclusion. "But there you were," she said, referring to my application, gesturing with her hand as if plucking a ticket out of a hat. I remember that same faculty singing the praises of my writing during a workshop and a classmate, another woman of color who had been a mentor to me at the time, called me that afternoon to say she didn't think the professor's praise was warranted because it only served to "pin us against each other."

When certain things happen to us, we wrestle. We ask ourselves, "is this tokenism or what?" At Mills College, it felt as if people of color were not supposed to be there, and it was natural for us to heap loads of pressure on ourselves to be better than the next person in order to achieve success.

•••

The banal call for diversity in literature isn't as glamorous and noble as we may believe. The writer treating on Christian themes is seldom invited to contribute her work or participate in any mainstream discourse—unless it vilifies the biblical institution.

I can only surmise that because the characters in our fiction walk the line of Christian faith, they are deemed irrelevant to the culture. They are "other" because their source of influence is reduced in society. Editors don't offer full disclosure as to why these literary pieces get cast out early, or later in the tier—they have feedback parameters in place. But when you read literary journals devoid of authentic Christian themes, a deficit is notable. It isn't because Christian writers are scarce—we do earn our MFAs after all.

It's unnerving that in the literary world—when it comes to matters of Christian polemic—depictions of morality and faith continue to be oversimplified or overlooked entirely. These treatments stump the work's full potential.

As a Christian who writes, what drives my creative work is to bring significance to the value of my faith. As a reader, I am intrigued by work that achieves this. Generally speaking, I look at Christian literature with a critical eye because most of what I've read in the mainstream that is tangentially religious is rife with superficial tropes and cliché and is mostly written by non-believers or outsiders. It isn't written right—there is no evidence of empathy, no suggestion of close observation. Most of it lacks dimension, most of it is a mere caricature. Thus, the story suffers, and the credibility of faith is jettisoned. It is easy to spot these inconsistencies, these failed attempts at depiction. Although characterizations may be substantiated in the story, the spiritual context, when it is diminished, alters its trustworthiness.

Critical thinking is necessary when handling this type of writing. References to faith ought to be taken seriously and editors would be wise to push this particular point further. Authenticity in literature is found wanting and the onus is on the writer to get it right—a hard sell to a secular editor. This critical thinking on Christian concepts is hard to find in contemporary literature—it requires work and publishers assume, potentially correctly, that readers don't want to do the work. They want to be entertained. They want to off-load analysis and symbolism to the workshop space, or to literary criticism—but not to publishing.

•••

Writers of color are not, generally, sought to speak at writers' conferences on topics that go beyond the ethnocentric, cultural themes. The mainstream astute gatekeeper looks for us to talk about the box we find ourselves in, centered around race and iniquity, and not on the topics of the writing process, the MFA experience, the craft of writing.

In her essay, "What White Publishers Won't Print," Zora Neale Hurston articulated the idea of gatekeepers keeping a tight lock on who gets access and who doesn't—it's uncanny how relevant her piece is today: "They know the skepticism in general about the complicated emotions in the minorities. The average American just cannot conceive of it, and would be apt to reject the notion, and publishers and producers take the stand that they are not in the business to educate, but to make money. Sympathetic as they might be, they cannot afford to be crusaders. In proof of this, you can note various publishers and producers edging forward a little, and ready to go even further when the trial balloons show that the public is ready for it.... The question naturally arises as to the why of this indifference, not to say skepticism, to the internal life of educated minorities."

She further declares, poignantly, where an answer to this indifference lies: "The answer lies in what we call the American Museum of Unnatural History. This is an intangible built on token belief. It is assumed that all non-Anglo-Saxons are uncomplicated stereotypes. Everybody knows all about them. They are lay figures mounted in the museum where all may take them in at a glance. They are made of bent wires without insides at all. So how could anybody write a book about the non-existent?"

Today, we're witnessing a hunger, so it seems, for us to penetrate the bent wires and dig out our insides, pluck out our heart from our chest so the world can see. Why a sharp, morbid interest now?

Hurston wrote: "The fact that there is no demand for incisive and full-dress stories around Negroes above the servant class is indicative of something of vast importance to this nation. This blank is not filled by the fiction built around upper-class

Negroes exploiting the race problem. Rather it tends to point up. A college-bred Negro still is not a person like other folks, but an interesting problem, more or less."

Hurston knew the extremities of racial bias and the undermining of the intellect when she described a slave master who stated that a teacher to a slave can "turn a useful savage into a dangerous beast."

It is disconcerting to imagine history repeating itself, subtly, in unsuspecting forms to the casual writer of color. We're put in categories of sales-worthiness. Our viability depends on the insufferable social media platform as the litmus test, lest we are passed up by the popular darling in the crowd of meet-and-greets at Christian Writers' Conferences.

Some of the most remarkable firsthand observations I'll never forget during my experience at a well-known (now defunct) Christian Writers' Conference in northern California came from gatekeepers.

•••

An agent, when I asked if he receives manuscripts from writers of color: "I do represent one woman of color already and I do get manuscripts from people of color, but they're just not good enough."

•••

An editor, when I asked if she would be interested in reading my proposal: "Do you know any influencers? How many follow you? I've heard your name before, but do influencers know you?"

•••

An agent, when I asked if my pitch was of interest to her: "You should consider starting your story by placing yourself say, on a beach, reflecting on the life you're about to share with your reader."

These conversations took place in 2017 and I'd like to believe a lot has changed in the span of four years. The reckoning would demand it so.

•••

In a lecture, the late Toni Morrison described good and evil and how it is dressed in contemporary literature: "Contemporary literature is not interested in goodness on a large or even limited scale. When it appears, it is with a note of apology in its hand and has trouble speaking its name. Evil is dressed up with a tuxedo and a top hat, while goodness lurks backstage and bites its tongue. Evil is constant. But you have to be an adult to consciously, deliberately be good—and that's complicated."

I realize that the fight for morality in literature is paper thin. In his essay "Why Is American Fiction in Its Current Dismal State?", Anis Shivani wrote: "The individual fiction writer would have to be strong enough to take the moral offensive against writing that deludes the reader into thinking that his private ignominies are worth celebration and memorialization. He must buck the trend by going against the monopoly on career rewards currently held by the writing industry (which for all intents and purposes blacklists and boycotts real outsiders, although of course the terms of the game can't be framed so bluntly), and by fighting the herd mentality of publishers whose interest is no longer to discover great fiction and build writers' careers, but who only want to replicate the last great sensation.... To come to writing from a strong moral position, some belief in universal values that makes one sleepless and distraught, will be like a fat, bald, ugly man crashing in on a slumber party of blonde supermodels."

Shivani is right. Taking a strong moral position is a disruption. Little is expected of novels because readers crave more vulgarity, more immorality, more profanity, and more cynicism. In a writer's forum, an author stated, "So many contemporary novels seem manic, agitated, escapist, goofy, fantastically un-serious, and concerned with nothing of lasting value."

The struggle of race has more appeal, it seems, to the gatekeepers at mainstream conferences, and maybe at Christian conferences as well, if at all. Hurston identifies this idea as the folklore of *reversion to type:* "This curious doctrine has such a wide acceptance that it is tragic. One has only to examine the huge literature on it to be convinced. No matter how high we may seem to climb, put us under strain and we revert to type, that is, to the bush. Under a superficial layer of western culture, the jungle drums throb in our veins."

For the Mexican-American writer, the experience seems to be limited and confined to one dominant narrative, whether echoed through our own voices, or other voices: the plight of migration across borders.

Literature and the gatekeepers have exploited the languishing immigrant type enough, courting it to the mainstream, reducing it to mere folklore. But to some of us who live the experience, either firsthand, or indirectly as a second-generation Mexican immigrant (as in my case), this archetype is not all we represent. Generations of readers are entertained by this theme—the tradition binds our stories as quaint, enshrining the Mexican-American writer to the immigrant experience, memorializing the plight of crossing borders, negotiating new languages.

Hurston knew that as artists, there was more to us than our ethnic identity. She wrote: "But for the national welfare, it is urgent to realize that minorities do think, and think about something other than the race problem. That they are very human and internally, according to natural endowment, are just like everybody else. So long as this is not conceived, there must remain that feeling of insurmountable difference, and difference to the average man means something bad. If people were made right, they would be just like him."

New York Times book critic Parul Sehgal examined book reviewers of the past whose critiques of writers of color were detrimentally flawed. We can confer her assessment of literary critics to literary gatekeepers. She writes about fluorescent condescension and stereotype, "the pleasant and dubious satisfaction of feeling superior to the past" and "the sensitive assessments" by critic John Leonard, who wrote: "American Indians do not write novels and poetry as a rule or teach English in top-ranking universities either. But we cannot be patronizing." She described a 1932 book review written by Elizabeth Brown about Countee Cullen's *One Way to Heaven.* Brown wrote: "Most of us have not yet reached the stage where we can appreciate any story about colored people at its face value without always straining to find in it some sort of presentation of 'Negro life.' It is, therefore, from one who frankly knows little about the subject, an impertinence to say that Mr. Cullen paints a convincing picture of life in Harlem but one can at least say that the picture is sometimes amusing, sometimes very moving, and at all times interesting."

As Sehgal critically examines the legacy of *The New York Times Book Review* and its critiques of writers of color, she asserts: "That's what these pieces do. They hover and mock, or patronize, the reviewer keeping his hands in his pockets all the while. He builds no case—he feels no need; the identity of the writer, the source of that obsessive fascination, appears to be all the evidence required for his scorn. We hear little of style, of argument or technique. They might stand in harsh judgment of the writer, but as examples of writing they're soft. They rarely quote the book or offer more than perfunctory summary...

Where Black writers are concerned, another pattern can be detected. Reviewers might impute cultural importance to the work, but aesthetic significance only rarely. And if aesthetic significance was conferred, it often hinged on one particular quality: authenticity."

It appears that work by a writer of color requires a literary critic to validate its authenticity. Moreover, gatekeepers are given license to object to the view of the world as it is observed through the eyes of the writer of color.

Toni Morrison sums up the effects of literary criticism: "My complaint about letters now would be the state of criticism. I have yet to read criticism that understands my work or is prepared to understand it. I don't care if the critic likes or dislikes it. I would just like to feel less isolated." Furthermore, Maxine Hong Kingston echoes a similar sentiment: "I don't mean they praise my work more, I mean that they understand what the work is about and there is more willingness now to read a book by a minority person and to criticize it as literature and not just see it as anthropology."

Until writing by people of color ceases to be viewed as a work of anthropology, its aesthetic value will diminish. Sehgal writes: "That presumption—that the work of the Black writer was always coded autobiography, and only coded autobiography—was so entrenched, it feels startling to see the Black novelist praised purely for technique and inventiveness, to see an artistic lineage located...."

Gatekeepers possess the keys that are inaccessible for the writer of color. I surmise that a good amount of writing has been incorrectly interpreted and underestimated for generations. One can't help but wonder at this time how many masterpieces of creative writing have been discarded, how many careers have been thwarted.

The presumption, however, that there is consensus among gatekeepers should be handled with care, by both the gatekeeper and the writer. If the industry is to reform itself by shedding its biases, its typecasting of writers of color, it needs to be contemptuous of gatekeeping and rethink who is made steward over the keys. Gatekeepers cannot be so pompous as to believe that they are omniscient agents and that readers are vacuous followers beholden to their leading them to the finest literature. Gatekeepers cannot underestimate the intelligence of readers, those intolerant of banal literature, by examining work with caution, possessing boldness and style in the process. When gatekeepers eschew the perpetuation of typecasting writers of color by acknowledging that we create art and have more to offer than a discussion about race in America, then we'll be called to speak at conferences, conventions, round tables, forums, and podcasts on the topic of our craft, and only when better criticism is written will we read books that go beyond type.

•••

The pursuit of publishing means bearing the burden of ethnic bias. Rather than continue to ponder what can be done, how this can all be reconciled, it is more urgent to define the present-day landscape of publishing. To be keenly aware of our position in the culture and discern what sets us apart, and to observe our environment and our behaviors, these become the edicts that measure our success in publishing.

But only Christ can unite. Christ brings a different reconciliation than what the world and culture proselytizes, through all our grievances, our shameful histories, and our oppressions. Fortunately, as believers, we are reconciled in Christ—equal members of God's household, as Ephesians states: "For he is our peace, who hath made both one, and hath broken down the middle wall of partition between us; Having abolished in his flesh the enmity, even the law of commandments contained in ordinances; for to make in himself of twain one new man, so making peace: And that he might reconcile both unto God in one body by the cross, having slain the enmity thereby: And came and preached peace to you which were afar off, and to them that were nigh. For through him we both have access by one Spirit unto the Father. Now therefore ye are no more strangers and foreigners, but fellowcitizens with the saints, and of the household of God" (Ephesians 2:14-19 KJV).

So when we see a new canon arise as a prescription to ethnic bias, we need to be skeptical. In lieu of being advised to seek the scriptures, especially Ephesians 2, we're prescribed a list of sociology books, texts that promise to increase our sensibilities and awareness about race in America.

I've seen Christians finish their prescribed reading repertoire only to receive applause for "having done their homework." Do they receive a gold star for learning about an ethnic people, examining them as specimens—anthropological texts to classify and exhibit on lists? Prescriptive approaches are a superficial antidote because what reading a book in the canon does is rigidly fix uniformity on a culture and removes individuality. People of color are distinct persons and are not a monolith, a stereotype, a collective. To say that you read and did your homework on the Mexican experience is not the solution to our racial woes; because as believers, we need to look only to the cross.

It's problematic to give permission for the canon to inform the Bible. The Bible is sufficient in all matters of faith and practice and is enough to sustain brotherhood and fellowship. The unity of Christ's body is what brings us together.

A few years prior to getting married, I attended a Spanish-speaking church. I got married in a Spanish-speaking church, I presented my firstborn child in a Spanish-speaking church, and when my husband and I decided to go to an English-speaking church, we did it with the intention of raising a family among brethren that represent the kingdom of heaven. We didn't want to isolate ourselves culturally in an ethnocentric church, but the paradigm shift came at a cost—mainly confronting unfamiliarity and tactlessness from English speakers who couldn't pronounce my name (a problem I certainly didn't have before), among other cultural and language differences. It was important for our growing family to thrive spiritually in a church that teaches sound doctrine and congregate in a biblically, family-integrated church that encourages fathers to lead the discipleship of their families.

We're at home in the presence of our multiethnic family in Christ, brothers and sisters who share a heavenly Father with us. We don't need a new canon of literature to help us build structures that will support or unite us, that will help us learn about each other. If we have Jesus, He is our cornerstone, and the unity of co-laboring with our brothers and sisters in the church body is all sufficient.

Eréndira Ramírez-Ortega
Writer & Creative Consultant

ON HERMENEUTICS AND POETRY

On Developing a Poetic Hermeneutic as a Cambridge Student

Jonathan Chan

IT WAS AS AN UNDERGRADUATE, while a member of the Christian Union of the University of Cambridge, that I first realized there might be an intrinsic connection between poetry and faith. Before that, the two had remained largely separate in my mind—I could appreciate Langston Hughes and Jack Kerouac, and delve into a Bible study with rigor. The notion that poetry could have a devotional orientation was still inchoate within me.

Those of us who were English literature students would often gather within the Christian Union, bringing our experiences of feeling misunderstood as the few Christians in the faculty. Our shared faith meant that we were usually the first to pick up on biblical references during supervisions, or better equipped to understand the psychological and even epistemic states of some of the writers we read: Milton in his blindness, Donne in his sickness, Julian of Norwich in her ecstasy. Other writers we knew to be Christians become touchpoints in our conversations—Gerard Manley Hopkins, George Herbert, R.S. Thomas, Shūsaku Endō. Their works provided a feeling of kinship, affirming that there were writers who expressed struggles over faith and doubt in their art. Reading poetry provided a generative space for contemplation and discussion, ambiguity and indeterminacy.

The group, however, did fall prey to the truisms of "loving God through loving literature"—we listened to talks held to think about Christian theories of reading or discussed theoretical moves grounded in Christian convictions. Looking back, it's clear that the notion that poetry had to be read through a lens of faith meant that poetry itself was instrumentalized, valuable only to the extent that it could be regarded as edifying. Never mind the fact that in scripture, as Robert Alter has argued, poetry was often chosen as a form to convey prophecies or express the voice of God because of its ability to conjure a sense of mystery through parallelisms.

•••

While in England, I witnessed attempts to integrate poetry into church services, sometimes as a prophetic truth-telling, other times to break monotony. Upon my return to Singapore, where poetry is not held in particularly high regard, the language of instrumentalization became sharper yet again. While conducting interviews for *Harvest & Wine,* a journal for Christians in the arts, it became clear that whether one was a sculptor or a poet or a filmmaker or a visual artist, the work was only ever seen as valuable if it was explicit in its evangelism. To read a poem only for its potential edification of the Christian self, or to offer a poem to another as a way of pushing forth the possibility of recognizing the Gospel, seemed to narrow the possibilities of poetry in and of itself.

This is not to say that faith has no place in the reading and writing of poetry. It is surely valuable to understand the spiritual or religious context in which a poet was raised to understand the metaphysics, the architectonics of their work. However, it is also vital not to allow faith to overdetermine how one reads a poem—glimmers of a sacramentality or religious iconography where there really is none. I learned this when I tried to link R.S. Thomas and Derek Walcott within a common fold of Christian spirituality for a dissertation. I was refuted on the claim that Walcott clung to any recognizably "Christian" definition of the transcendent. His was more oceanic and beatific than pietistic and liturgical. It was not enough for me to pick up on references to biblical narratives to try and make a case for religiosity in a certain tradition—nor, really, was it a particularly fruitful exercise.

•••

The reading of poetry is a necessarily hermeneutic act—few other literary genres possess such a pronounced sense of contrivance and craft. This contrivance is most noticeable at the level of the line, whether it is enjambed or metrical, rhyming or loose, and it is here where poetry most firmly differentiates itself from its counterparts. This attention to craft can mask the moment of faith from which a poem often germinates. However, one does not read a poem in order to make a judgment that a poet believes in that which they have written. Nor should one read a poem as an exercise in determining a set of beliefs, whether religious or political. To do so is to withhold from the poet the dignity of complexity, the ways in which poems can open up new vistas of thought in the imagination, whether that leads one to contemplate the transcendent or the immanent, the abstract or the concrete, the chronological or the kairological. Sometimes a poem is straightforward, other times it is mystical and mysterious, lending itself to or resisting interpretation, whether within a recognizably "Christian" framework or not.

A poet I see as taking on a mystical position is A.R. Ammons. The critic Daniel Hoffman has remarked that Ammons's poetry "is founded on an implied Emersonian division of experience into Nature and the Soul." The idea of Ralph Waldo Emerson's pure, unadulterated perception of nature is present in Ammons's poem "The City Limits" (1986), which an acquaintance has described as an "atheist hymn." Yet, this imputed reading feels like a disservice to Ammons's depiction of the generous, all-encompassing nature of "radiance." As he writes:

When you consider the radiance,
    that it does not withhold
    itself but pours its abundance
            without selection into every
    nook and cranny not
            overhung or hidden
    [...]
    the heart moves roomier, the man stands
            and looks about, the
    leaf does not increase itself above the grass,
            and the dark
    work of the deepest cells is of a tune
            with May bushes
    and fear lit by the breadth of
            such calmly turns to praise.

There is a clear sense of the numinous at work here—the sense of mysticism woven through the poem, of the interconnections within the touch of this radiance, revealing a beneficence without invoking a specific deity. To Ammons, this light touches "air or vacuum, snow or shale, squid or wolf, rose or lichen" without prejudice. It is enough to create a change within the speaker's "heart," a radical act of cosmological flattening as "the / leaf does not increase itself above the grass," and cosmological concordance where "the dark / work of the deepest cells is of a tune with May bushes." There is something of the mystery of faith in this poem, one that does not aim to identify specific religious categorizations.

If a mystical orientation in poetry can feel depersonalized, turning to poems that examine faith as generationally transmitted may be helpful. In particular, the poems of Li-Young Lee and Boey Kim Cheng provide examples of how faith lingers through familial memories. This is salient, given that both poets are of Chinese heritage, though Lee is American and Boey is Singaporean Australian. Filial piety remains an embedded moral instinct for many in the Chinese diaspora. Lee's poetic self is best understood biographically—his father served as personal physician to Mao Zedong, his family moved to Indonesia then fled owing to Sinophobic sentiment, then they arrived in the United States after interludes in Hong Kong and Japan. After settling in Pennsylvania, Lee's father went to seminary, eventually becoming a Presbyterian minister. It is through the elder Lee, a mythic figure in Lee's poetry, that faith emerges as something inherited and contradictory; in "Mnemonic" (1986), the younger Lee writes:

> A serious man who devised complex systems
>   of numbers and rhymes
>   to aid him in remembering, a man
>   who forgot nothing, my father
>   would be ashamed of me.
>
> Not because I'm forgetful,
>   but because there is no order
>   to my memory, a heap
>   of details, uncatalogued, illogical.
>
> For instance:
>   God was lonely. So he made me.

My father loved me. So he spanked me.

It hurt him to do so. He did it daily.

The speaker recalls a father whose memory is precise and systematic; the speaker is utterly incapable of replicating his father's rationality. The syllogisms that follow indicate the illogic of his memory—"God was lonely. / So he made me.", "My father loved me. / So he spanked me." Their parallel structure intuits a link between the speaker's father and God, united in the contortions necessary to understand love as creation and as violence; love as discipline and as confusion. Faith thrums beneath generational difference, an expression between discipline and disorder. There is a confluence of the Confucian ideals of punishment and the distorted biblical view of how the person "who spares the rod hates his son," as stated in Proverbs 13:24. Faith is not pristine, for it is tarred by a most intimate violence.

For Boey, his speaker's relationship with faith is problematized in a different way—the poem "Clear Brightness" (2016) introduces a speaker for whom a generational transmission of faith has ceased. The poem reads:

> Now grave news from the living I have left;
>   the cemeteries are dug up, razed, the dead
>   expelled, their bones unhoused, ashed
>   and relocated to columbaria to make
>   room for progress. No more tomb-sweeping
>   and picnicking with the dead.
>
> No such unrest for Grandma and Dad
>   who went straight into the fire.
>
> Anyway they turned Catholic
>   and have no use for paper money
>   or earthly feasts.

Boey's poem proceeds from an encounter with Australian bushfires. The sight of "raining embers" activates a memory of the Qingming festival, a Chinese tradition where families visit the tombs of ancestors, clean their gravesites, make offerings, burn joss sticks and paper, and pray to them. In Singapore, graves were exhumed so cemetery land could be repurposed for public housing. The remains of the dead were cremated, put into urns, and moved into columbaria. Boey brushes this aside with the line, "Anyway they turned Catholic"—many Chinese abandon such ritual practices upon their conversion to Christianity. Boey's speaker is lapsed in both faiths, distant spiritually and physically from Chinese folk religion and Catholicism. His poem is not strictly theological but considers the transcendent, the emotive power of memory, as well as living as a migrant, holding tradition, faith, and embodied memory in tension.

The poems discussed so far have held an explicit articulation of faith at a remove. However, when the names of other biblical figures are invoked, one can no longer be so evasive. Lucille Clifton's "slaveships" (1996) features recognizably Christian names and archetypes, yet she wrestles with their multiple meanings and connotations. Clifton's "slaveships" proceeds from the cruel irony of such names being given to the eponymous ships:

> Jesus
>> why do you not protect us
>> chained to the heart of the Angel
>> where the prayers we never tell
>> and hot and red
>> as our bloody ankles
>
> Jesus
>
> Angel
>> can these be men

who vomit us out from ships
called Jesus Angel Grace of God
onto a heathen country

The invocation of the names "Jesus," "Angel," and "Grace of God," hollows out each of their meanings, both through repetition and their juxtaposition against dehumanization. The reference to Ezekiel in "can this tongue speak / can these bones walk" has a prophetic, salvific dimension, as does the visual allusion of Jonah spit up by the whale with the slaves "[vomited]" out from ships. Clifton displays a hostility toward the hypocrisy of Christianity as weaponized in the slave trade, but not necessarily Christianity itself. To Clifton, these names of God are rendered in the fullness of their contradictions, an act that need not be regarded as either pious nor faithless.

•••

Perhaps where it is most relevant to think of the place of faith in reading a poem is when it feels inherent to the action of the poem itself. This sort of faith does not need be expressed merely through Christian verbiage, but may be read as an everyday persistence. It is this expression of faith that has most moved me in such poems as Spencer Reece's "ICU" (2010). In "ICU," the ideas of faith as resilience and as devotion to God are entwined. This is, in large part, a result of Reece's own dual vocation as poet and priest, yet there is a subtlety to how faith operates in his writing. It is not as ebullient as Hopkins, nor as explicit as Herbert. It postures toward the mystical, is lucidly aware of its own limits, and finds itself present amid fraught circumstances. The poem is grounded in Reece's experience in hospital chaplaincy.

While its beginning sets up an expectation that the poem will deal with violence wrought upon Black bodies as seen from an ICU, the poem turns instead to a neonatal ICU. Reece approaches this with delicacy, illustrating the fragility of each child in the unit. The speaker notes:

> A Sunday of themselves, their tissue purpled,
>   their eyelids the film on old water in a well
>   their faces resigned in their see-through attics,
>   their skin mottled mildewed wallpaper,
> It is correct to love even at the wrong time.

There is an existential precarity conveyed through the discoloration and thinness of the skin, translucent and fragile. The rejoinder, that "It is correct to love even at the wrong time," reads not with a moralistic smugness about a chaplain's role, nor as an exercise in self-justification. It seems a statement of conviction, of the necessity that love should persist even amid great fear and potential despair. Yet, while Reece could have ended the poem in this way, he continues, offering agency to the infants who "eyed me," the chaplain doing rounds. The infants are likened to "Orpheus in his dark hallway," who says: *"I knew I would find you. I knew I would lose you."* The ambiguity and italicization of these lines are chilling. Is the chaplain the Eurydice to the infants' Orpheus? Have they already entered a kind of afterlife, a form of Hades? Is the chaplain drawn into this liminal purgatory that the infants fighting for their lives already inhabit? The poem advances from the quotidian and routine to the precarity of infant life, elevated through myth. The lines conjure the sense that faith persists and operates even in the face of the painfully unknowable.

When Reece came to speak at a class in which I was enrolled, I felt a great kinship with him, not only through the poems that he read but also his admission that he's not always conscious of what goes into his writing of a poem. There was a great humility in admitting this. It is something I often feel when I write my own poems too. Unless the conceit of a poem I work with is explicitly pietistic—about prayer or fruits of the spirit or something else that could be glossed as devotional—the poem emerges out of some festering of thought or feeling: a moral, mental, emotional, or psychological discomfort. Often these discomforts are tied to particular intuitions that stem from my faith.

Yet, I have come to the slow realization that while I would be thankful if someone made their way to God through a poem of mine, what has become more important to me is writing with a kind of integrity, or a kind of truthfulness, writing with an honesty that is self-aware and not evasive. Faith itself is only as expansive as our own perceptions—to share something of it in the reading and writing of poetry is difficult, vital, and not always to be presumed.

Jonathan Chan
Poet & Author

IN THE ABSENCE OF ECSTASY

Rachel Seo

IT WAS THE FEAR OF HELL, actually, that drove me to Jesus. One night when I was eight, I squeezed my eyes shut and begged God to come into my heart in a desperate attempt to avoid the Bad Place. I continued to do this dozens of times over the course of the next several years: at Christian youth events, family-friendly magic shows sponsored by local churches, evangelical concert tours and music festivals put on by 95.9 the Fish. Every time, I walked in trying to feel something, and when I joined the streams of people walking into the venue—girls wearing cutoff jeans shorts that ended at the knee, kids hoisting cheap backpacks weighed down with twisty fish pins—I thought I did. I liked the idea of joining a mass migration moving upward toward heaven. The feeling of standing beside so many people united for one purpose felt, to me, like the presence of God.

But when the altar calls ended and the curtain dropped, I always slid back into a subliminal state of doubt. Salvation at those points was a dream—insubstantial, fading in tandem with the emotional high. I became increasingly dubious when I realized that I experienced similar feelings in unholier places: at public high school assemblies, when my classmates and I sang the alma mater together and our words strung a thread-thin connection between our isolated selves for a few halting seconds. When I went to concerts at tiny venues in Los Angeles, twisting to avoid the gyrating couples grinding on each other while simultaneously letting the music carry my psyche to the clouds, I knew in those moments that much of the pathos of modern American evangelicalism can be easily imitated in the swell of a chorus of voices.

JIA TOLENTINO ON ECSTASY

This has always haunted me, but I couldn't quite quantify it until I read an essay by *New Yorker* staff writer Jia Tolentino called "Ecstasy," in which she chronicles her de-conversion from Christianity. Reading it for the first time felt like peering into my own head, even though the two of us eventually emerged into different spaces. "I've been walking away from institutional religion for half my life, fifteen years dismantling what the first fifteen built," she writes. In her narrative, drugs and Jesus, church camp and hip-hop form a dizzying concoction that melds the ecstatic with the apostatic. She recalls swallowing pills "crushed into Kleenex" and then going to a concert, where she "felt weightless, like [she'd] come back around to a truth that [she] had first been taught in church: that anything could happen, and a sort of grace that was both within you and outside you would pull you through." Ecstasy, in this case, refers to both the drug and the spiritual state of mind—suggesting, implicitly, that they are one and the same, but that whether you believe that or not, there's beauty in being drawn outside of yourself.

Further along, she presses against the memory of her past, writing, "I can't tell whether my inclination toward ecstasy is a sign that I still believe in God, or if it was only because of that ecstatic tendency that I ever believed at all." One of the unspoken questions in this is that if drugs mimic the ecstatic joy that religion is supposed to give us, why is religion necessary or important?

But I suspect the essay is about much more than that. It's a testimony of de-conversion, the antithesis to the Christian's testimony of faith. Both kinds of narratives are personal with evangelistic undertones, but not explicitly persuasive. "Ecstasy" forced me to think about why Tolentino chose to leave Christianity—and, inversely, why I choose to stay.

WHY I CHOOSE TO STAY

For me, the answer ends up being something vague and undemonstrative. Some believers can identify a moment of transformation, a lightning bolt that brought them to their knees. But what happened to me was an accumulation of smaller moments. I was sitting in math class one morning, surrounded by numbers and words volleying back and forth from the teacher to the class, my classmates to me, when in the midst of the dialogue I found myself confronted by the idea of a fork in the road, a clear binary that demanded to know where I stood and why. I hated math because it felt sterile and demanding in a way that was both presumptuous and narrow—you were right or you were wrong, and I hated being wrong—but perhaps that was how I began to understand: I could either walk completely away, or swivel toward the light that had been blinking at me for so long. When I tried to read my Bible at night, I always came back to the book of Ecclesiastes. "Remember also your Creator in the days of your youth," it reads, "before the evil days come... before the sun and the light and the moon and the stars are darkened and the clouds return after the rain, in the day when the keepers of the house tremble, and...the grasshopper drags itself along, and desire fails, because man is going to his eternal home." Instead of reviving my fear of hell, the verses brought to life my understanding of what I define now as constancy. Faith sometimes comes not in flashes of light, but rather in a slow dawn. One day you might wake up to its brilliance shining in your face and understand it as reality, becoming absorbed into it, fully, by the all-encompassing wholeness of grace.

Tolentino, too, describes a wholeness—but hers is a kind of limited enclosure, one sprung from the stifling experience of attending one of Houston's megachurches. Spun throughout her essay is an increasing lack of trust in the power structures that propped up the faith of those around her, an awareness of the duplicitousness and hypocrisy that lay under the enormity of her church. The Christians she knew, she writes, valued wealth as "divine anointment" and acted like "they were worth more to God and country than everyone else." In that context, the cultural, the political, and the biblical feel one and the same, all of them standing on equal footing. To be one meant to be all three: an unholy trinity. Threads impossible to detangle.

This is, in fact, one of my favorite parts of the piece, how the narrative structure parallels the story itself. It unfolds slowly, winding the reader down a lazy river, a drifting, but still linear, narrative. But if Tolentino's faith has unraveled to the point of its nonexistence, the unraveling of my own has helped me see the individual threads that comprise it more clearly.

A NEW PRECISION

More recently, I've had a growing desire for greater precision within the language of my faith—a process of detangling various definitions and winnowing the lines between faith and religion, American evangelicalism and Christianity. I, too, wonder about institutions: how to fight against their inherent flaws, how to deal with the disappointment of their failures. I wonder about what I don't know: what it means to grow up apart from where I am, how the cultural context of my life affects the way I glorify God with it.

It's forced me to think at a more molecular level, too, picking through assumptions and applying Bereanic levels of energy in an attempt to understand not only what it means to be a Christian, but a Christian *now*. Where I find myself standing, though, is with the knowledge that these questions test my faith in ways that allow me to chip away at the excess until I'm left with the truth. And the Gospel, as truth, will hold up against the circumstances of the here and now, because it simply states what is. Knowing that the notions of glory I caught in flashes when I was younger have actual hardiness under the glitz; that the human nature is something I can and can't accept at the same time; that the staggering sin which exists within ourselves and our organizations is evident, oh so evident, in the ways we walk and talk and breathe and live—this exists in me as simultaneously crashing waves of aching and joy, because it's personal. And the personal gathers itself into the collective, and indeed the collective, categorized as "the whole creation" in Romans 8:22, "has been groaning together in the pains of childbirth until now."

It's this pain that makes me marvel both at the fundamental inconsistency within our sin condition and, in contrast, the continuation of the Gospel truth that acts as its foil, destroyer, and savior. If my younger self sought constant flight, my present self finds peace on solid ground. After all: grace runs deeper still.

Rachel Seo
Writer & Student

YIELD YOURSELF TO ART

On the Film Drive My Car and the Invitation to Criticism

Micah Rickard

> You must become the person who is willing to change your life based on the exhortations of art.
>
> **A.O. Scott**

LIFE AND ART ARE FAR TOO INTIMATE to settle for imitation. Art is born of life; in turn, life is informed and reformed by art. Every work of art leaves us with a choice as to how we will be shaped by it, but the reality that we will be shaped by it is never in question. This reality confronts us with some pointed questions: In what ways will our lives be shaped? In what ways do we even *want* to be shaped? How does that affect our forms of engaging with art? Each question adds a layer of intention to the way we understand and engage with works of art.

This dynamic invites us into new forms of participation and imagination, and to participate with clarity and purpose, to care about art and how it shapes us. It's an invitation to criticism—not the criticism that we often (wrongly) associate with insular reviewers, but criticism as a cultivated, everyday way of being. Criticism is the reciprocal act of our encounter with novels, films, concerts, paintings. We should consider this invitation and purposefully join alongside art in the dynamic of our own formation.

•••

This interplay between art and personal formation suffuses *Drive My Car*, a film by Ryusuke Hamaguchi that observes the intimate, interweaving flow of grief, connection, and hope, all swept up within the current of art's transformative power. It's a long and tough film—but also one that finds a calm, substantive touch, trusting simple framing to express the emotional murkiness that its characters swim in. The camera—and the story—keeps the characters generously in frame, so long as they want to be. In the moments when they want to fade from sight, the film gives them that space, drifting to seascapes and mountainsides.

In *Drive My Car*, art is always near. Yusuke Kafuku is a successful actor and theater director preparing for a new production of Chekov's *Uncle Vanya*. Kafuku's wife, Oto (Reika Kirishima), is a screenwriter, and theirs is a marriage animated by story: she mystically crafts stories in an ecstatic state after sex, and Kafuku recounts them the next day to aid her writing; conversely, he memorizes the lines for his plays by using tapes that Oto records, with her performing the parts opposite him. But the comforting rhythm of their partnership doesn't last for long. After a delayed business trip, Kafuku returns to his apartment to find Oto in a stranger's erotic embrace. Not long after, he walks through the same door to find her dead on the living room floor. The first event rends their relationship, but the second causes it to vanish.

All of this is only the prologue, the stage that Hamaguchi sets, as *Drive My Car* stretches and settles to a calm pace that belies its devastating heart. Two years on, Kafuku is incapable of moving beyond these twin tragedies. Preparing for another production of *Uncle Vanya*, the tape becomes his way of crystallizing Oto's presence and confronting her for her infidelity. He drives, he practices his lines, he accuses, he memorializes, and he subsists.

But his ritual and aching solitude are disrupted as he travels to Hiroshima to direct his new production. The first rupture comes as a loss of agency—his contract mandates that he be given a driver, even if he continues to use his own car. The second comes through the provocation of his cast. Made up of men and women of varying nationalities, each performing in their own language, the cast is nonetheless of one accord in how they prod and pull Kafuku out of his routine. Some do so with warmth, some with unflinching immediacy, but they gradually force Kafuku to confront his loss. Janice Chan (Sonia Yuan) pricks against his rigid approach to rehearsals. Lee Yoon-a (Park Yurim), a woman who speaks using Korean Sign Language, shows Kafuku an unfamiliar level of kindness. But the sharpest challenge comes from Takatsuki (Masaki Okada), a young, self-interested star—and one of Oto's former lovers.

As time goes on, his grief compounds with the pains of his driver, the reticent Watari (Toko Miura), who's evading her own tragic past. The two are hardly capable of expressing these intimate pains to others, let alone living fully with them. But even as they're confronted by their inability to fully reckon with their past, art offers a path forward.

As his driving ritual is interrupted by the presence of Watari (and more forcefully by Takatsuki), Chekov's lines begin to carry new meaning. Subtly but irrevocably, these words give Kafuku the means to weep, to lash out, to rage, and to calm. Just as *Uncle Vanya* gave voice to his confrontation of Oto, so it gives him a language for confronting his grief—even if those words aren't his own. It also gives him and Watari space to acknowledge each other and to share the burdens that have weighed on them both for so long.

•••

Art holds a generative power, revealing ways of being that were otherwise unknown to us. Through Hamaguchi's characters, we begin to see the multifaceted ways we relate to art: hiding beneath it as an escape, throwing ourselves into it in search of heightened experience, blindly being shaped by it, or yielding to it with purpose. But we do more than just watch— we also participate.

As we encounter works of art, we join in practices of hope and grief, of perseverance and lamentation. The dividing line between character and audience is always a tenuous one, and Hamaguchi shows us that we are always actors, always weaving our experiences into the narratives we encounter. We are invited to make the drama our own in some sense. In the process, we "put on" the characters' emotions and "perform" their responses.

And so we participate with Kafuku as he processes the remnant of his pain, slowly coming to terms with Chekov's encouragement that "we'll patiently endure the trials that life sends our way." Only as he enacts this arc of perseverance does he find a way through his own tragedy. Perhaps, as we join with him, we will also learn to live amid our own trials.

Adding to this, *Drive My Car* shows us that we need to be moved by and toward others for this dynamic to fully bear fruit. As long as Kafuku is trapped within himself, art is merely a means for escape. Despite years of reciting Chekov's lines, he's no closer to forgiving his wife or himself. He's no closer to moving beyond his tragedy. It's not until he's forced to enter into the play with others that he recognizes a new possibility, not until the sacred space of his car is shared by Watari that the words begin to have meaning within relationship.

The transformative capacities of art are expressed and enacted communally, and even cross-culturally. Even if Kafuku's actors don't speak each others' languages, the repetition and communal participation slowly changes them. Art doesn't merely shape our ways of being; it shapes our ways of being *together.* The provocations, encouragements, and generosity of others are necessary for Kafuku to be able to appropriate Chekov's redemptive power for his own life. Likewise, it's only as he acts *toward* others that those changes are truly realized.

•••

In the midst of this arc of redemption, there's also a note of warning that must be addressed: The transformative power of art is not necessarily a beneficial one. As Kafuku tries to coach Takatsuki (who's taking Kafuku's typical lead role), he gives him a portentous challenge: "Chekov is terrifying... It drags the real out of you... Yield yourself." Such an exhortation is meant to bring out a truer performance, but it echoes forward in ways more violent than Kafuku intends. After their conversation, Takatsuki chases down and beats a man who tried to take his photo; a short time later, while rehearsing a scene in which his character tries to shoot another, the police arrive to arrest Takatsuki for murder. The mirror between the acted play and real events is intentional—Takatsuki does indeed yield himself, but his character is only further disfigured.

We cannot afford to be naïve. Art is seductive, and its power bears an inherent danger, which Tara Isabella Burton discusses in an essay for *Aeon* titled "Dark Books." (Burton is here focused on reading novels, but her points can be reasonably extrapolated to other forms of narrative.) Burton points out that, as we yield to art, it "can erode at our sense of self." Following Kierkegaard, she imagines the storyteller as a vampire who "infects a person's sense of self and drains his life force by means of corroding influence." If art, at its most intimate, constitutes a relational encounter—a thing we *can yield to*—then it follows that we return from such an encounter having given something of ourselves, having gained something, or having been marked by something. Otherwise, it would not be a true encounter—at least not an intimate or powerful one.

Burton's metaphor of the vampiric capacity of novels can be carried further: the encounter leaves one not merely "infected," but gradually and expansively transformed, such that one becomes an entirely new creature. As art reveals newly possible ways of being—and especially as it invites us to participate in them—it reorders our desires, thoughts, and practices. Over time, this reordering has the potential to imperceptibly change us into radically new people.

•••

So where do we go from here, if art is vital to our lives, yet bears the capacity to either form or deform us? I believe the situation reveals two things: first, a need for redemptive art; second, and more crucially, a need for intentional criticism. It would be easy to focus on the former, calling for works that depict only clear arcs of positive growth. But to do so would severely limit the multitudinous capacities of art. Not all art is redemptive, nor does it need to be. Some works find vitality in satire. Others intentionally aim at the destruction of idols that have been blindly praised for too long. Still others leave redemption hinted at in the negative space of the story. The critical, satirical, and deconstructive modes of art can't be cast into the outer darkness—we need these works as much as any others.

This guides us to the second revelation—the need for perceptive, rightly grounded reflection and criticism. And, if all modes of art are indeed vital, then this exhortation bears even more weight.

The call to criticism is not a call to a lofty ideal, but an intentional, daily way of being. As *New York Times* critic A.O. Scott writes, "It's everyone's job, and I believe it's a job we can actually do." He further clarifies that our response to a work of art is an exercise of freedom, and the aim of criticism is "to figure out what to do with that freedom." We can be formed in dialogue with art as we carefully reflect on it; or we can be blindly moved by it, with no regard for the direction it takes us. In this way, Kafuku and Takatsuki act as guides along each divergent path.

Our reflection must be perceptive, by which I mean nuanced, discerning, and aimed. Without nuance, we are prone to overlook the mode that a given work is operating in. If we mistake satire for positive description, we may leave the encounter *mis*shapen; if we interpret provocation as prescription, we will dismiss a work outright, missing the good that it offers us. We must also be discerning, seeking to identify the new ways of being that a work creates. And we must always have an aim, a *telos*—an idea of how we want to be formed. What values do we want to cultivate, or what ways of being do we want to reject?

Similarly, criticism must be rightly grounded. We walk into any museum or movie theater with a complex web of stories that have already shaped our understanding of the world and of story itself. We are not only potentially formed by this new encounter; we are always already formed by the stories we've previously encountered. We must understand this grounding, for by it we posture our encounter for this new story, whether that leads us to accept or reject, to interrogate or blindly adhere.

This is particularly vital for People of the Book, people whose lives are fully grounded in a specific story that gives us both ontology and *telos*. We have a narrative—and a reality understood by that narrative—against which we inevitably measure new stories. Some stories hearken to this arc, encouraging us to recall God's truth in ways direct or oblique. Other stories may critique us, often pointing to ways we have failed to live in accordance with Scripture. A cultivated perception and right grounding work together to orient the practice of criticism. Cultivated criticism—whether in response to a twenty-minute sitcom or three-hour Japanese movie, a brief poem or *War and Peace*—practiced as an everyday way of being can be a powerful tool for formation.

We are always in the midst of transformation, even as it moves in the undercurrents of our experience. Even as it ever erodes what we thought was impenetrable about us. *Drive My Car* is expansive and patient enough to bring such subtle movements into relief. Kafuku's grief is enfolded within layer after layer of memory, performance, literature, and language, until it all unifies into a desperate, redemptive whole.

Drive My Car is a film of stillness, even as we move in time and place. It's also a story of our subtle, meaningful transformation, even when we feel we're stuck. To use its own phrase, it extends into "an amplified silence." As the film concludes, a final scene of Chekov's play is performed wordlessly, as Lee Yoon-a incorporates Kafuku himself into her sign language. It is a momentous embodiment of art's immersive, communal, and cross-cultural power to reform us.

"Yield yourself." Despite the inherent danger, Kafuku's instructions still call us into this imaginative play, albeit with a deeper awareness of the invitation and call. For we must go a step further than he acknowledges: We are not ever only actors, we are also always critics.

Micah Rickard
Writer & Engineer

BEING TRANSLATED

R.M. Wilcher

ON THE TABLE, THERE IS A BOOK, Jean-Louis Chrétien's *Loins des premiers fleuves,* lying open to a poem which has no name. I've simply given it the designation "Untitled Nine." In the second line, there is a verb which, in English, has no equivalent. That is not to say that any word when invited over from one tongue to another ever forms a one-to-one equivalent, especially given that every language has intimacies known only to those who root themselves within its particular hospitality, like the curtain folds of my childhood home in which I once enshrouded myself. But this word is particularly tricky. It could mean one of two opposite actions: either *to scatter* or something in the range of *to gather, to collect,* or *to count.* It could mean all of it once. Chrétien has purposefully placed the verb within a context (an image of dust in the wind) which offers little clarity. I have opted to translate it as to gather because *to collect* has a permanence which *to gather* does not. Things collected are more likely intended to be stored up and horded away; things gathered can be scattered again in the wind.

My translation reads,

Without end the dust
gathers the sudden
lapses of wind

I have no guarantee that my rendition is the best; in fact, I know it isn't. To *count* would be the most literal. But I have tried to leave open its ambiguity, the possibility of its opposite, and attempted to land somewhere in between all of its possibilities. I am translating the one in order implicitly to include the others, and in so doing I navigate its *between-ness*. Translators are often navigating a word's between-nesses, perpetually at play in a "broken middle" (to appropriate poorly a term coined by the late Gillian Rose) between words—inviting, coaxing, wooing sense across the expanse of the impossible, interpreting infinitely other intimacies. It is an act which is never wholly complete, and yet the end result is hopefully a readable translation. A translation is itself something of a *between*. It is at once the original and an image of the original, these words but not, at once *res* (the thing itself) and *signum* (the sign), an *alter ego*, never quite wholly either. That is really how everything in the world is—at least that is what Platonists like myself tend to think; the world exists as a *between*. A translation is a new world, and the world is a translation of divinity.

To understand what I mean, it may require one once again to take up the imagination of ages past, an imagination which is more or less lost to us now. The Church Fathers (and Plato before them) imagined our world as metaphysically situated in between formless nothingness and the infinite fullness of being, the Good Itself, or God. Finite being, sung out of nothing, was the gift of participation in the Triune God. In every case of particular entities, in the life of each and every thing, this participation could been seen and understood: a narcissus flower never ceases to be a narcissus flower (a sign that it is upheld in the mind of God, per Saint Augustine, by the eternal idea of narcissus-ness), and yet it undergoes change, buds, blooms, withers, and dies (a sign of its finitude and frailty, its incapacity to encompass that idea totally in itself). It is *imago narcissus* in the way that we humans are *imago Dei*. Every narcissus realizes in part the superabundant possibility of the original, and each strives repeatedly to realize this idea deeper and deeper.

Every narcissus "repeats differently" the same eternal idea of narcissus-ness in the way a translation repeats differently the original words of another language, so says the Anglican metaphysician Catherine Pickstock. In this frame, this narcissus here is a kind of translation of the infinite into the finite. It does not close off the infinite but, on the contrary, opens out the finite into the infinite and even brings the infinite intimately closer to the finite. That is why the 19th-20th century French philosopher Maurice Blondel can write, "I walk beneath the weight of the infinite." Where a thousand narcissus flowers lie along a hillside, each unfolds the original's superabundant possibility ever and again anew. In this way, not only is the world as a whole a *between* and a repeating differently of its eternal original in God, but so are each and every thing in the world. Every little thing is a world unto itself, singing back its own harmonious intimacy to the God who is more present to it than it is to itself.

•••

Our various arts and forms of enquiry are explorations of the various between-nesses of these worlds within our world. Each art and science is directed ultimately, and whether or not such disciplines are aware of it, to the Original from which they derive their being. The brunt of modern science is a navigation between physical causes (usually chemical and electrical) and their effects. Depending on who one asks, philosophy is (crudely) a navigating between terms and claims to truth or else (even more crudely) a navigating between the self and the world. Theology is the science or art of navigating between God and humanity. The art of translation navigates between words in one language and another. Admittedly, I am not sure what sort of *between* it is that poetry navigates, but painting is a bit more apparent. The painter explores the *between* of images and

215

their originals, between the painted narcissus and this narcissus among a thousand others which bursts white and pink along a single undulation of hill. Various styles and forms of painting navigate the between-ness of things differently, touching along various aspects of the originals, just as various methods in the sciences can treat differently the same essential objects. The original does not have to be something material in the world (the narcissus), for abstract expressionism and especially the works of Wassily Kandinsky (I think especially of his *Composition X*), along with entire traditions of religious art are there to remind us that the spiritual is also there to be painted, translated into terms which the unversed can more easily, or at least intuitively, grasp.

If everything is "between" and every art is a navigating the between, then to be true to the task of art, the artist must stand in a place between everything. The genius of the artist is not mastery of skill (nor the skill of mastery) but the un-mastering of her voice and vision to a middle place between things, mediating one thing to another. She becomes *middle-voiced*, both active and passive, both the giver and the recipient of form. Those who have ever experienced what is called "inspiration" are no doubt familiar with this sense that one is both making and merely instrumental in a higher making, and being thus the artist feels oneself made, unmade, remade in a moment. Still, the artist lends her voice to both poles of between-ness, to the copy and the original, to the finite and the eternal, in order that they can speak their intimacies, their belonging to each other. And it is not simply to each other that they speak.

By mediating their silent voices, the artist addresses this speech to the lovers of art and the lovers of the things navigated. This, I think, is why Russian literary critic and sophiologist Vladimir Solovyov can speak of the artist as a prophet. The artist whose voice middled is a prophet of the between and therefore a real prophet, a prophet of the real. Allowing art and reality to speak their belonging to each other, as ambiguous and broken as that belonging remains, is the spiritual task of art. However, in the modern period, we have mostly failed to retrieve again (to repeat differently, if you will) the imagination of the Fathers, and therefore, especially in the case of René Magritte and his much praised *The Treachery of Images*, this task has often been scorned in favor of irony.

•••

Magritte's infamous *This Is Not a Pipe*—among his others, which lay the modern framework for both oxymoronic virtual reality and the idea of the internet meme—transfigures ambiguous belonging into a rationalist's clarity of unbelonging. The painting depicts what might ordinarily appear to be a common tobacco pipe with the caption *cesi n'est pas un pipe*. The pipe painting does not allow the image and the original to speak their belonging to each other; instead, Magritte speaks for them. His *n'est pas* ("is not") sets the image of the pipe over and against what a pipe really is and thereby sets art over and against reality. He clarifies the essential ambiguity of the *between* of art (where harmonious wonder ought to spring up and water parched lands surrounding), and he makes it a no man's land between trenches, beating one side down with artillery shells of irony. Magritte's work is a severing of the repetition of things and signs the dehiscence of reality itself. It scorns the hospitality of the real, attempting an escape into the *sur*-real—more accurately, the *sub*-real. The painting is translated right out of the world. It should be said, however, that Magritte has mistaken irony for the truth itself, the ultimate double irony, and it is only when irony is mistaken for truth itself that art can produce the virtual. Irony, after all, is a sign of some implied truth waiting to be revealed.

Other attempts have been made to clarify or even explain away the betweenness of art. I think particularly of American minimalism in the 1960s with its goal of eliding all referential power in the objects of art. Where surrealism sought to disconnect *signum* from *res,* minimalism sought to erase the *signum* altogether, to do away with art's capacity to speak at all. For minimalism, the objects of art held no reference to other forms. This square did not belong to other squares or sign the meaning of squareness. It was simply *there.* There is no intimacy to translate, only brutal shapes in space. And thus, the infamous phrase by one of minimalism's foremost figures, Frank Stella: "What you see is what you see." Reference, however, is irreducible. It was Agnes Martin, whose own work stands to this day between minimalism and abstract expressionism, who signaled minimalism's ultimate failure to elide reference which, for those of us who can appreciate a movement for its failure, is its greatest achievement. Martin's navigation through the *aporia* left in minimalism's wake opened her out into a Platonist and Augustinian appreciation of beauty in everything, especially friendship.

•••

It was in Kettle's Yard that I discovered the between-ness of things for myself. The wonderful art museum curated, and once lived in, by the Edes is one of the great testaments to art's ineliminable capacity to sing its participation in the real, and ultimately in God. Jim and Helen Ede transformed their own home into an art gallery in the late nineteen-fifties and made it open to the public. Every room navigates the between of things by intentionally placing workaday household items amongst the art that hangs on walls and rises from dining room tables. The art, in turn, beckons its welcome to the mundane things. For example, in the living room, Joan Miró's surrealist painting *Tic Tic* has a small yellow sphere in its lower right corner; on the coffee table along an adjacent wall, a lemon (which is replaced every week by the current museum staff) rests in a little bowl.

The yellow sphere in the painting spells the real yellow lemon, and thus what was meant to escape the real is suddenly ever more enfolded within it, and I stand somewhere between them.

I, as an art viewer, must navigate the real space of the house in order to allow its between-ness to come to full bloom in my bodily perceptions and in my very soul. I am called to respond to, and even somehow participate in the art by moving about the Ede's home. In a bedroom, David Jones's magnificent *Vexilla Regis* hangs behind an open door. In order to see the painting properly, I must get somewhat behind the door and in the way of everyone coming in and going out of the room by it. In order to see it, I go on a kind of quest like the one for the Holy Grail toward which the painting itself gestures. To take up the quest by moving about the room is no longer to remain a mere "art viewer," a perfectly detached modern subject cut off from my own participation in the world. Participating in the art as its observer (as its witness), I renew my belonging in the world. As I sat in a chair in that room with *Vexilla Regis,* I became translated back into the real with all my little intimacies previously unknown even to myself.

I return again to my translation. The reasons for leaving the ambiguity of the verb unclarified have, I hope, become clear. To pick one pole or its opposite, both abundantly possible meanings, would be to do what Magritte did with his pipe or what the minimalists did with their structures—it would be to neglect the intimacy and the belonging of art with reality and the belonging of reality in God. I am trying to put my little voice in the middle of all of that fray and ineliminable possibility as best I can manage, and while it is not capable of doing it perfectly, in attempting it I discover yet another voice, some helper singing along beside me, some inner teacher guiding my muddled words.

To translate these words on the page from French to English, I am no longer an unencumbered observer, a mere pair of eyes hanging above the white ground where the words happen. I, too, am suddenly translated, or perhaps *transfigured* into a participant in the real through the mediation of art. I am walking through the Ede's house. I am, for lack of a better term, *transubstantiated* (for who is it really that is being devoured in the Eucharist?). I take this body and bread into me, but I am also incorporated into a Body. Through art, as through the Eucharist, I become transfigured into what I have always already been: intimately within the folds of the curtains of the world, filled with light.

Nothing ever escapes the middle; I don't know why anything or anyone would want that. To escape the real is but to drift into nothingness, *scattered* into the void rather than *gathered* into fullness, gathered "to a greatness, like the ooze of oil / crushed." Art, like everything which is here for a moment and, like Chrétien's dust in the sudden lapses of wind, is gone the next, nevertheless beckons us to gaze infinitely deeper within and out beyond the world. From the vantage of this broken middle which we artists and enquirers inhabit, art is a witness that our desire for God outweighs the world by absolutely affirming the world, so that everything, especially ourselves, might be transfigured into glory, translated into the intimacy of God.

R.M. Wilcher
Writer & Academic

THE DEPTH DIMENSION

Matthew Lawrence Campbell

ALL I REMEMBER IS THE COLD—that and how tired I felt as an eight-year-old trekking through the forest. "In the interest of time," my dad had said, "we should probably cut through this bowl here, as opposed to trying to circle around it. We might even get lucky and flush something out while we're at it. What do you think, Matthew?" I don't exactly remember what I said in reply.

The previous night had seen to it that Arizona's White Mountains, that sprawling vastness of alpine plain and rising peak situated atop the state's northeastern plateau, received their first official snow of the year, and I had emerged from my tent earlier that dawn to behold a world utterly transfigured in white...not to mention about 30 degrees colder for it.

But of course, we weren't there for the winter views, beautiful as they were. Rather, we were perched atop that ridgeline somewhere in the middle of the Arizona wilderness, binoculars dangling about our necks and shotguns at the ready, on the hunt for wild turkey. We had been roughing it for days by then and with absolutely no sign of them. Not so much as a single footprint from among the fallen leaves or tangled bramble to season our wandering with prospect and aim. In my worst moments, I had even begun to wonder whether the whole trip wasn't some kind of cruel ruse on the part of Powers who enjoyed subjecting unwitting eight-year-olds and their fathers to long days of pointless striving. But that day felt different. Cold and tired as I was, something about the way the rising sun broke soft and clear through the snow-laden trees lent the morning a special air of renewed hope. Confidence, even. We took a moment to pause. To take in the grandeur of the waking world around us. To savor its magnitude and scope. And then we were off...

•••

The topic of "art and faith" has always struck me as somewhat odd. For as fashionable and animated as our discussions about it are today, throughout most of human history, the vast majority of people on this planet, regardless of which God or gods they happened to believe in, would likely never have thought to consider the matter. Now, it's not as if cultures of the past never bothered to reflect upon such things as the meaning of art and beauty and their relation to ultimate reality, but when it comes to art and faith as definable ways of life—as concrete "modes" of "being in the world"—most would have simply taken it for granted that the two not only fail to contradict each other, but in fact constitute natural extensions of the same living whole. Among Christians, for instance, there would have been no hard and fast distinction between the spiritual message of the Gospel, on the one hand, and the creative exertions of the Church's many painters, illuminators, architects, composers, and sculptors on the other. That one should have to struggle to reconcile the two would thus have been as outlandish a prospect as it would have been just plain inconceivable, simply because the Way of Jesus and the Way of Beauty flowed self-evidently from a single source—God's own Self.

I say this, because I think it's important to appreciate just how much our collective wrangling with and enthusiasm for this issue in modern times is contextually determined—a function, that is, of the attitudes and assumptions that lie at the heart of our culture's current conception of reality. Difficult as it is to imagine from our modern cultural lens, there was a time when the cosmos positively dripped with divine agency and intent. All that is, visible and invisible, mundane and sublime—from the patterned course of the stars to the structure of society, from the ordering of the seasons to the most intimate stirrings of the soul—all bore witness in some fashion to the presence and unifying power of the numinous. Reality, you might say, was like a marvelous tapestry: dazzlingly variegated and complex, but also harmoniously proportioned and teleologically imbued.

But things are much different now. By and large, we tend to envisage creation as a cold, inert, and arbitrary thing. More a random assemblage of lifeless mechanical parts than anything else. For the most part, we probe and dissect creation as if it were an anonymous cadaver on the examination block, not a miracle in whose secret depths the inscrutable lineaments of a Face flash forth.

•••

The Prussian sociologist, Max Weber, was the first to assign this shift in perspective a name and to put it to rigorous use. Since the scientific revolution and the emergence of an industrial, bureaucratized social economy, he argued, Western culture has fallen prey to a gradual process of "disenchantment." In our collective efforts to rationally decode the natural world and bend it to our will, we've simultaneously stripped it of its "primal magic"—its inherent capacity to elicit an encounter with the Divine via reverence and awe. Deprived of this crucial "depth dimension," creation is now a barren and hollowed-out semblance of its former self. From the vantage point of an additional hundred years on Weber, I would only add that it's become a terribly *fragmented* and *alienated* one, as well. All our technological and scientific progress over recent years, in other words, has come at a high price: estrangement from ourselves, each other, the natural world—from the ground of Being itself. And no number of digital distractions, trips across the world in search of "authentic experiences," or craft IPAs can ultimately hide that fact, much less dull the pain left in its wake. We are isolated and adrift like never before.

In a way, then, the modern age amounts to one long test case in what a universe without a transcendental source for its unity, stability, and identity invariably comes to look like: the dismemberment of life's "whole" into compartmentalized, self-enclosed parts; the proliferation of unnatural dualisms and antagonisms; the desperate clinging to rigid forms of certainty in order to counteract a mounting sense of one's meaningless-ness and anxiety; contempt for the body and of material order more generally—in short, everything breaks apart and unrav-els. Not even the church, which is supposed to operate as a sign of a healed and divinized humanity, has proven immune. For who can deny the presence of many Christians today, espe-cially here in America, who would seem to equate orthodoxy with the adoption of an attitude of suspicion, if not outright hostility, toward a "Godless" outside world? Such Christians like to make a great display of their principled stance against the erring course of secular society without stopping to consider that, in doing so, they often dispense with one of the central pillars of the Gospel's message, namely, that God's creative activity, goodness, and beauty are at work everywhere and at all times—not just within the insular hold-outs of their church communities. Since orthodoxy in their construal is less a living, breathing thing than a reductive list of answers to pre-formu-lated questions, anything smacking of novelty or surprise—the events and developments of history, recent cultural trends, and new insights, for example—is reflexively branded a potential source of contagion, something to fear. Naturally, the irony here is that, precisely in its reactive posture toward modernity, much of what passes for "orthodoxy" today ends up looking and behaving every bit as modern as the next thing.

In any case, when it comes to art, it seems to me that the clearest indication that disenchantment has infected a Christian's soul is when she experiences a knee-jerk impulse to want to "christianize" any form of art that doesn't immediately present itself as "christian."

Unsurprisingly, the results of her endeavors usually end up being a painfully forced mixture of both kitsch and portentousness. Which is to say, they lack the mark of true, lasting works of beauty, because they proceed from the faulty (and thoroughly modern) assumption that the natural and the supernatural are fundamentally separate—as opposed to inextricably inter-braided—discourses. You'll recall that the hallmark of a disenchanted mind is the conviction, however unstated, that creation has ceased to be a locus of Theophany, a conduit of the Divine Life and Presence in whose image it was self-evidently made. For the Christian wanting to make art, this implies that a poem or a painting can't *just* be about the flowers on the windowsill, or the sound of women laughing through the lemon trees; it has to be *explicitly about* God in order to precipitate an encounter with Him. Left to themselves, the sights, sounds, and smells of our mundane experience are at best deficient, and at worst downright threatening. The believer, therefore, has to come in after the fact and supplement them with an extrinsic layer of spiritual subject matter if they are ultimately to amount to anything.

•••

After about 20 or so minutes of picking our way down the mountainside, Dad and I emerged from the pine, out of breath and coated in needles, reaching a clearing at the bottom of the bowl. Just opposite, about 50 feet on, stood a grove of aspen decked out in full autumn splendor. As we stepped over the boundary, though, it was more as if we had stumbled unaware into the heart of some massive fire. Save for the white bodies of the aspen themselves standing everything about us was a riotous conflagration of reds, oranges, and yellows. Morning mist rose like smoke through the tree-trunk colonnade in graceful *grand adages* of holy praise. It seemed to me then that we had chanced upon a secret the forest must have been guarding, so quiet and so pristine was the stillness that enveloped us. Still technically on the hunt, our feet traversed the leaf-down forest floor, but all thought of turkey had long since fled our minds...

We never did manage to bag a turkey on that hunting trip. Chalk it up to inexperience or just plain bad luck on my part. But amidst the silent stature of those aspen trees, I had been gifted something far greater and more enduring. Something which, though it only lasted only a few moments, has been grafted into my blood, seared into the marrow of my being, for all time. And I thank God for it.

•••

I'd like to suggest that the problem we Christian artists encounter today—this seemingly unbridgeable divide many of us experience between our faith and creative lives—is in large measure an artificial one. That's not to say it isn't serious or doesn't warrant our attention. But what it does mean is that it needn't be there. We can change it if we want to. But that, in turn, requires a willingness on our parts to go inward. We have to summon the courage to recover within ourselves an authentic love of mystery, a genuine openness to the unpredictability, risk, and play of existence. Put differently, we need to remember that the starting point of any orthodoxy worth its salt will always be the eternal mystery of the Incarnation, the act whereby God leaves the security of His Trinitarian abode to take on not only the flesh of our humanity, but also the flesh of all created being, thereby wedding it to Himself for all time. Indeed, to the incarnation-grounded orthodoxy, each tree, each blade of grass, each flash of thrush-wing among the briarwood participates in the Redemption. Each thing of beauty, whether man-made or natural, has a place marked for it in the Kingdom to come and yet already and mysteriously in our midst. Such an orthodoxy accustoms the eyes of the believer to view creation through the lens of Genesis 1—that is, as "very good." Doubtless, creation is wounded, subject to death and sin, pain and suffering—but "very good" all the same. And precisely because of this "very good," it still retains the indelible stamp of its Creator. In its inviolable core, the Wisdom and Beauty of its Creator still burn softly, silently, like hearth-ember. Far from stifling the vital impulses at creativity's ground, then, true orthodoxy can and should enhance them.

Matthew Lawrence Campbell
Writer & Poet

ABOUT EKSTASIS

EKSTASIS IS A CREATIVE PROJECT by *Christianity Today,* aiming to revive the imagination and foster a community that sees the poetic side of life and faith.

FIND MORE AT

ekstasismagazine.com

ABOUT

SEA HARP PRESS

Sea Harp is a specialty press with one overarching aim: in the words of Andrew Murray, to "be much occupied with Jesus, and believe much in Him, as the True Vine." Our mission is twofold: to reinvigorate the Church's reading of the best of the past, and to bring out fresh editions of both today's and tomorrow's classics — all for the purpose of personal encounter with Jesus Himself.

For every piece of media we consider publishing, we ask two fundamental questions:

- Is this work entirely about the person of Jesus of Nazareth?
- Would the Early Church have thought this work worthy of sharing?

We take our name from the original Hebrew word for the Sea of Galilee—*Kinneret*: כִּנֶּרֶת: meaning "harp"—which was given because of the harp-like shape of the shoreline around which Jesus ministered. It was, in less words, a place known as the Harp-Sea.

Thank you for joining us as we walk the Way with that most wonderful Man of Galilee.

the
SEA *of*
GALILEE

W W W . S E A H A R P . C O M

SEA HARP TIMELESS

Other books in the series